SpringerBriefs in Computer Science

SpringerBriefs present concise summaries of cutting-edge research and practical applications across a wide spectrum of fields. Featuring compact volumes of 50 to 125 pages, the series covers a range of content from professional to academic.

Typical topics might include:

- A timely report of state-of-the art analytical techniques
- A bridge between new research results, as published in journal articles, and a contextual literature review
- A snapshot of a hot or emerging topic
- An in-depth case study or clinical example
- A presentation of core concepts that students must understand in order to make independent contributions

Briefs allow authors to present their ideas and readers to absorb them with minimal time investment. Briefs will be published as part of Springer's eBook collection, with millions of users worldwide. In addition, Briefs will be available for individual print and electronic purchase. Briefs are characterized by fast, global electronic dissemination, standard publishing contracts, easy-to-use manuscript preparation and formatting guidelines, and expedited production schedules. We aim for publication 8–12 weeks after acceptance. Both solicited and unsolicited manuscripts are considered for publication in this series.

**Indexing: This series is indexed in Scopus, Ei-Compendex, and zbMATH **

Linan Huang • Quanyan Zhu

Cognitive Security

A System-Scientific Approach

Springer

Linan Huang
New York University
Brooklyn, NY, USA

Quanyan Zhu
New York University
Brooklyn, NY, USA

ISSN 2191-5768   ISSN 2191-5776   (electronic)
SpringerBriefs in Computer Science
ISBN 978-3-031-30708-9   ISBN 978-3-031-30709-6   (eBook)
https://doi.org/10.1007/978-3-031-30709-6

This Springer imprint is published by the registered company Springer Nature Switzerland AG
The registered company address is: Gewerbestrasse 11, 6330 Cham, Switzerland

Preface

Humans are indispensable components in Cyber-Physical Systems (CPSs) due to their cognitive capacities and the ultimate goal to support rather than supersede humans. The close integration of humans, CPSs, and Artificial Intelligence (AI) creates AI-Powered Human-Cyber-Physical Systems (HCPSs) that drive the development of Industry 5.0 and revolutionize the future of work. Despite the remarkable cognitive capabilities (e.g., situation awareness, decision-making, and cooperation) of human users, operators, and administrators in designing, operating, supervising, and securing HCPSs, humans have been the weakest link in HCPS security.

Attackers are increasingly sophisticated in exploiting not only vulnerabilities in software and hardware but also human vulnerabilities to obtain initial credentials from human users through phishing, scamming, and various types of social engineering. These exploitable human vulnerabilities lie primarily in human cognitive processes such as perception, attention, memory, and mental operation. An adversary can use a variety of reactive (e.g., design deceptive phishing emails to evade users' attention) and proactive (e.g., generate excessive feints to overload human operators) methods to disrupt human cognitive processes so that humans misperceive the HCPS state and/or are misled into fallacious reasoning and incorrect decisions. The consequence can exacerbate and further lead to the compromise of cyber and physical components, as well as a system-level meltdown. It is both opportune and imperative to create socio-technical solutions to break such a cognitive kill chain, make humans resilient to cognition-based threats, and enhance the *cognitive security* in the new battle field of HCPSs.

To this end, in this book, we present a *system science foundation* that builds on and bridges the fields of psychology, neuroscience, data science, decision and game theory, and learning theory to develop transdisciplinary *socio-technical* mechanisms at the convergent human-technology frontier to mitigate cognitive threats. Based on the understanding of human cognition and multidimensional data from various biosensors, this book develops *human-centered assistive AI technologies* to improve cognitive resilience and harden cognitive security. Leveraging system-scientific approaches to cognitive security brings quantitative, modular, multi-scale, and transferable solutions. This book goes further to create new metrics and characterize the fundamental limits of cognitive security.

The book investigates emerging cybersecurity concerns regarding human cognition and behavior and does so from a unique system perspective. It provides a self-contained introduction to the area of cognitive security and a succinct overview of essential system-scientific methods that play a central role in the modeling, analysis, and design of human-centric security solutions. The book uses reactive and proactive attention attacks as two case studies to demonstrate the system-scientific modeling and design of assistive solutions. Cognitive security is a multi-disciplinary and vibrant area of research. The chapters of this book are not meant to be comprehensive, but they are organized to offer readers an overview and several success stories that will motivate future research in the broad area and push the frontier of human-technology convergence.

The authors of this book would like to acknowledge their association with the Center for Cyber Security (CCS) at New York University (NYU) when a major part of this book was completed. We both like to take this opportunity to thank many of our colleagues and students for their input and suggestions. Special thanks go to members of the Laboratory of Agile and Resilient Complex Systems (LARX) at NYU, including Zhiheng Xu, Jeffrey Pawlick, Juntao Chen, Junaid Farooq, Rui Zhang, Tao Zhang, Yunhan Huang, Tao Li, Shutian Liu, Yuhan Zhao, Yunfei Ge, Yunian Pan, Patrick Yubeaton. In particular, Patrick has helped with proofreading of this book, and his suggestions have drastically improved the quality of the presentation of this book. We would also like to acknowledge the funding support from the National Science Foundation (NSF), the US Department of Energy (DOE), and the Army Research Office (ARO).

Brooklyn, NY, USA   Linan Huang
Brooklyn, NY, USA   Quanyan Zhu
December 2022

Contents

Acronyms

AI   Artificial Intelligence. 1–5, 13, 16–20, 44, 46, 51–53, 70, 90, 93, 97, 107
AoI   Area of Interest. 70, 72–74, 80
APT   Advanced Persistent Threat. 6, 62, 103, 107

BO   Bayesian Optimization. 71, 78, 80, 83

CDF   Cumulative Distribution Function. 30, 31
CPS   Cyber Physical System. 1–5, 7, 12–14, 17, 19, 20, 42, 44, 45, 51, 56, 87, 90, 103, 104
CPT   Cumulative Prospect Theory. 28, 30, 31, 56

DDoS Distributed Denial-of-Service. 12, 13, 92
DoS   Denial-of-Service. 87, 88

EUT   Expected Utility Theory. 28–31, 56, 57

HCPS Human-Cyber-Physical System. 1–3, 5, 7, 11, 14–21, 27, 31, 34–36, 45, 46, 48, 51, 52, 57–62, 87, 103–105, 108–110
HMI   Human Machine Interface. 4, 12, 13, 17
HRA   Human Reliability Analysis. 14

IDoS   Informational Denial-of-Service. 8, 11–13, 16–19, 21, 55, 87–93, 95, 98–100
IDS   Intrusion Detection System. 15, 35

Chapter 1
Introduction

Abstract Human cognitive capacities and the needs of human-centric solutions for "*Industry 5.0*" make humans an indispensable component in Cyber-Physical Systems (CPSs), referred to as Human-Cyber-Physical Systems (HCPSs), where AI-powered technologies are incorporated to assist and augment humans. The close integration between humans and technologies in Sect. 1.1 and cognitive attacks in Sect. 1.2.4 poses emerging security challenges, where attacks can exploit vulnerabilities of human cognitive processes, affect their behaviors, and ultimately damage the HCPS.

Defending HCPSs against cognitive attacks requires a new security paradigm, which we refer to as "*cognitive security*" in Sect. 1.2.5. The vulnerabilities of human cognitive systems and the associated methods of exploitation distinguish cognitive security from "*cognitive reliability*" and give rise to a distinctive *CIA triad*, as shown in Sects. 1.2.5.1 and 1.2.5.2, respectively. Section 1.2.5.3 introduces cognitive and technical defense methods that deter the kill chain of cognitive attacks and harden the cognitive security. System scientific perspectives in Sect. 1.3 offer a promising direction to address the new challenges of cognitive security by developing *quantitative, modular, multi-scale, and transferable* solutions. Figure 1.1 illustrates the structure of Chap. 1.

Keywords Cognitive security · Cognitive reliability · Human-cyber-physical systems · Human-centered AI · Cognitive attacks · Cognitive vulnerability · Cyber security · Data science · System science · CIA triad

1.1 AI-Powered Human-Cyber-Physical Systems

Cyber-Physical Systems (CPSs) are "smart systems that include engineered interacting networks of physical and computational components", as defined by the National Institute of Standards and Technology (NIST) in 2017 [30]. Despite the increasing automation and intelligence in CPSs, humans play indispensable roles in accomplishing CPS tasks, as illustrated by the mission stack in Fig. 1.2. The rapid development of Artificial Intelligences (AIs) and big data has facilitated a

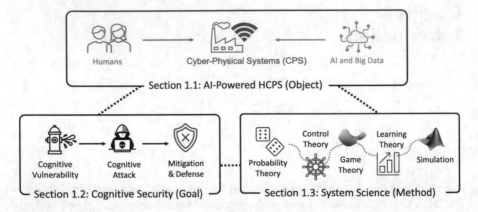

Fig. 1.1 The structure of Chap. 1. AI-powered HCPS in Sect. 1.1, cognitive security in Sect. 1.2, and system science in Sect. 1.3 are the object, goal, and method of this book, respectively

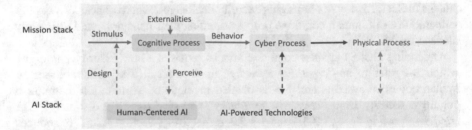

Fig. 1.2 The overview diagram of human roles and AI-powered technologies in CPSs. The mission stack at the top illustrates the task-driven flow chart that consists of human, cyber, and physical processes in green, blue, and yellow, respectively. The AI stack at the bottom illustrates the AI-powered technologies that interact with the human-cyber-physical process to assist with mission completion. To achieve human-centric objectives, AI-powered technologies need to *perceive* the process and outcome of human cognition and *design* additional stimuli to guide human cognitive process, as illustrated by the down- and up-side green dashed arrows

close integration of AI-powered technologies along with the mission completion, as illustrated by the AI stack in Fig. 1.2. We will elaborate on the human-involved mission stack and the AI stack in Sects. 1.1.1 and 1.1.2, respectively. The structure of Sect. 1.1 is illustrated at the top of Fig. 1.1.

1.1.1 Human Roles in Mission Stack

Humans *cannot* and *should not* be superseded in CPSs. First, due to their distinguished cognitive power and analytical capabilities (e.g., logical reasoning, symbolic abstraction, knowledge transfer, understanding of others' intent and emotions, etc.), humans have been playing irreplaceable roles, including determining demands, designing mechanisms, and responding to incidents. In addition, the inevitable progress of "Industry 5.0" [23] has reemphasized human-centric solutions to create personalized products, services, and experiences. The increased level of automation aims to *support* rather than *supersede* humans.

The mission stack in Fig. 1.2 summarizes the system-level integration of human touch with cyber and physical processes, referred to as Human-Cyber-Physical Systems (HCPSs), for mission completion. After a human participant receives a stimulus, he processes it and outputs responsive behaviors that influence the cyber and physical processes. The cognitive process can be affected by externalities related to individual factors (e.g., personality, awareness, and expertise), environmental factors (e.g., workload and stress), and social factors (e.g., peer pressure and culture).

Human participants have different roles (e.g., users, operators, security analysts, and administrators) in mission completion, and the associated cognitive process can take different forms. Two examples are provided as follows.

Example 1   End users, including employees and contractors, use the provider's computing facilities to maintain the corporation's normal operations. For example, the stimulus for employees could be working emails. Their cognitive processes affect the accuracy and timeliness of the phishing[1] recognition, which results in either secure behaviors or falling victim to phishing.

Example 2   Security analysts investigate alerts in real time for alert triage and response. The alerts, the triage process, and the response are the stimulus, the cognitive process, and the behaviors, respectively, in this alert management scenario.

More details of cognitive capabilities and human roles in mission stack of HCPSs can be found in Chap. 3.

1.1.2   Incorporating AI Stack into Mission Stack

The advances in AI have accelerated the automation and smartification process in cyber and physical layers, as shown by the blue and yellow double-headed arrows in Fig. 1.2. AI has been widely applied to sensing, control, communication, and data processing in a variety of applications such as biomedical monitoring, robotics systems, and digital twins [24, 31, 65, 71]. In these CPS applications, AI not only serves as a technology for reasoning, planning, learning, and processing, but also enables the manipulation of physical objects. For example, autonomous driving cars

---

[1] Phishing is coined as a combination of the words "password" and "fishing" to describe the practice of tricking Internet users into revealing sensitive data, including passwords.

adopt AI to sense the environment (e.g., road condition, weather, and the movement of pedestrians and other cars) and determine the optimal driving setting (e.g., speed, brake, and steer). AI-powered technologies in these CPS applications should be scalable [4] and transferable [59].

Compared to *technology-based* AI design that enables humans to adapt to technical systems, *human-centered* AI aims to design systems that are aware of human cognitive processes to augment human perception, cognition, and decision-making capabilities in the rapidly evolving, complex, and uncertain CPS environment. Besides the desirable features of scalability and transferability for AI-powered technologies, we further require human-centered AI to be *customized, explainable, ethical, respectful of privacy, and trustworthy*. Such requirements are based on a thorough understanding of the human cognitive process and fulfilled by designing proper human-assistive technologies (e.g., Human Machine Interfaces (HMIs)), as shown by the downward and upward green dashed arrows in Fig. 1.2, respectively. The detailed design of human-centered AI should be adaptive to CPS applications of different functions, features, requirements, and constraints, as illustrated by the following examples of driving-assistive systems and power grid HMI. The perception and design, as illustrated by the downward and upward green arrows, can contain different aspects depending on the application.

Example 1   The basic function of a driving-assistive system is to accurately and timely perceive the traffic condition and evaluate whether the driving behavior is appropriate under the current condition. Besides the *perception of external conditions and behaviors*, a driving-assistive system needs to further perceive the driver's mental states, including attention levels and emotions, through biosensors. These *perceptions of the internal cognition state* can aid in the prediction and prevention of inappropriate and insecure behaviors. For example, an increased heart rate or body temperature may indicate road rage, and certain precautions should be taken (e.g., limiting the car speed). In addition, a driving-assistive system needs to be *explainable* to facilitate trust and minimize a driver's decision time to take proper action [10]. For example, the HMI should not only display the recommendation but also the reasons and supporting evidence.

Example 2   Besides the perception aspects of AI illustrated in autonomous driving, AI-enabled HMI in the control room of a power grid should further learn from user behavior and feedback because grid operators are well-trained experts capable of evaluating the AI assistant's answers and providing feedback. For the display design, it should support efficient invocation and dismissal because the number of actions an operator can do in a time window is limited, especially in a time-constrained environment [56].

1.2 Cognitive Security in HCPS

CPSs have been under threat of various attacks since their emergence. Established on the mission stack and the AI stack illustrated in Fig. 1.2, we incorporate the attack and defense stacks in Sect. 1.2.1 to form the four-stack dissection of HCPS security, as illustrated in Fig. 1.3. After the above panorama of HCPS security, we zoom into the focus of this book, i.e., cognitive process, cognitive vulnerability, cognitive attack, and cognitive security, in Sects. 1.2.2, 1.2.3, 1.2.4, and 1.2.5, respectively. The structure of Sect. 1.2 is illustrated at the left bottom of Fig. 1.1.

1.2.1 Attack and Defense Stack

Figure 1.3 illustrates the vertical dissection of HCPS security, including the attack stack and the defense stack in orange and gray, respectively. In the past decade, attacks have evolved to be *targeted, intelligent, multi-staged, and multi-phased.* The typical life cycle of these attacks consists of the following four stages. In the reconnaissance stage, attackers gather intelligence to determine the attack goal and identify vulnerabilities in the target network. In the planning stage, attackers tailor their strategies to the selected vulnerabilities and choose attack tools. In the execution stage, the attackers deploy the malware to gain an initial foothold, expand access, gain credentials, and escalate privilege. Finally, the attack in the

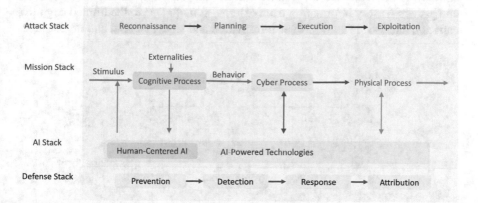

Fig. 1.3 The vertical dissection of HCPS security consists of attack and defense stacks over the mission and AI stacks. The four orange boxes in the attack stack illustrate the typical life cycle of an attack. First, attackers tailor their attack strategies and select attack tools in the planning stage based on the reconnaissance results (e.g., exploitable human and technical vulnerabilities). Then, an attack is launched and inflicts damage in the execution and exploitation stages, respectively. As illustrated by the four gray boxes in the defense stack, a typical defense consists of four stages: prevention, detection, response, and attribution

exploitation stage exfiltrates confidential data, interrupts cyber services, or inflicts physical damage.

The four gray boxes in the defense stack illustrate four defensive courses of action. The prevention stage includes the precautionary and proactive defense methods used in advance of attacks. Intrusion prevention techniques, including firewalls and demilitarized zones (DMZ), may be ineffective, especially for advanced attacks such as Advanced Persistent Threats (APTs). Therefore, intrusion detection and response are necessary to protect against them. Featured-based [77] or anomaly-based [47] detection can be applied at clients and servers to analyze the network traffic flow and identify malicious behaviors. Depending on the detected attacks, the response methods include applying associated patches, isolating the malicious IP address, and restricting the access privilege. Besides these *reactive* detection and response methods, honeypots can *actively attract* attacks and detect attacks with a low false-positive rate. In the meantime, by *actively engaging* with the attacks, honeypots delay the hacking process. The attribution stage includes post-event analysis, threat intelligence acquisition, and an accountability system.

1.2.2   Feedforward and Feedback Cognitive Processes

Figure 1.4 provides a zoomed-in version of the dynamic cognitive process that consists of feedforward and feedback processes, represented by solid and dashed arrows, respectively. We first illustrate the feedforward cognitive process, where the stimulus is the input and the behavior is the output. First, sensation [7] decodes and gathers sensory information from external stimuli. Due to the limited cognitive capacity, attention is used to filter information and store essential and urgent items

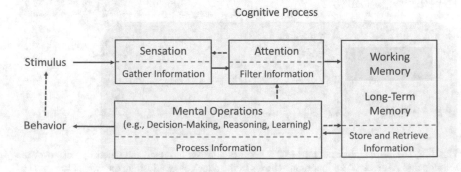

Fig. 1.4 A zoomed-in version of the cognitive process that includes sensation, attention, memory, and mental operations: The feedforward path in solid arrows illustrates the information flow of gathering, filtering, storing, retrieving, and processing. In the feedback loops, behaviors alter future stimuli, mental operations affect LTM and attention, and selective attention determines sensation, respectively, as illustrated by the dashed arrows

in working memory. Then, humans process the information for mental operations, including decision-making, reasoning, and learning, which subsequently lead to observable behaviors. Based on the tasks and scenarios, human mental operations may need to retrieve past experiences that are stored in the Long-Term Memory (LTM). The cognitive process also includes several feedback loops listed below:

- Behaviors have an impact on the CPS and change the subsequent stimulus.
- Mental operations learn new knowledge and store experience in the LTM.
- Besides passively filtering the collected information in the feedforward process, attention also actively affects sensation by directing our awareness to relevant stimuli while suppressing distracting information. Such *selective attention* [46] has been demonstrated in phenomena such as the *cocktail party effect* [3].
- *Selective attention* is a result of the mental operations and is usually goal-driven and endogenous (referred to as the *top-down attention*), compared to the *bottom-up attention* that is endogenously driven by the stimuli.

1.2.3   Exploitable Cognitive Vulnerability

Each component of the cognitive process in Fig. 1.4 possesses distinct vulnerabilities exploitable by attackers [19]. We discuss vulnerabilities concerning sensation, attention, memory, and mental operations in Sects. 1.2.3.1, 1.2.3.2, 1.2.3.3, 1.2.3.4, respectively. We refer the readers to Chap. 4 for a detailed review of system-scientific approaches to analyze, exploit, and mitigate these cognitive vulnerabilities.

1.2.3.1   Vulnerability of Sensation

Sensation is a complex process that involves visual, auditory, somatosensory, olfactory, gustatory, and vestibular systems. These systems follow patterns that can be exploited by attackers. For example, knowing the sensation limits (e.g., it takes around 150 and 200 ms on average to see [5] and hear [26] a signal, respectively) and contributing factors (e.g., how light, color, and noise affect human sensation), attackers can create environments where humans are prone to sensation errors. Human sensation systems can sometimes undergo distortions of the senses (e.g., visual and auditory illusions) and produce false sensory information. By understanding the contributing factors and causes of these sensory illusions, attackers can craft phishing websites and emails with fewer identifiable phishing indicators.

Besides exploitable patterns and illusions, human sensation is also susceptible to manipulation. Attacks have adopted many psychological techniques, including *priming* [58], to manipulate sensation in HCPSs. Priming is a well-known phenomenon in psychology wherein the presence of a stimulus impacts how later stimuli are processed or interpreted (e.g., humans recognize the word "food" more quickly after the presentation of the word "kitchen" than the word "office") [54]. The majority of priming is positive and increases the sensitivity of the related stimulus, while negative priming [76] slows down the processing speed. Both *positive* and *negative* priming can be weaponized for sensation hacking. For example, attacks may use positive priming to emphasize certain ideas in phishing or use negative priming to de-emphasize the phishing indicators. Based on whether the stimulus is consciously perceptible or not, priming is classified as *supraliminal* and *subliminal*, respectively [25]. Due to its stealthiness, subliminal priming can be a primary candidate for sensation hacking. As shown in the experiment results [42], by subtly presenting words or images that are physically or semantically similar to the judgments preferred by the attackers, attackers can influence the accuracy or false alarm rate of the inspectors.

1.2.3.2   Vulnerability of Attention

Attention can be described as an overall level of alertness or ability to engage with surroundings [54]. Humans rely on attention mechanisms to control their limited computational resources in the brain for maximum information acquisition. Despite the remarkable success of human attention, it suffers from reduced performance under multitasking, long duration, stress, fatigue, and heavy cognitive load. Moreover, as a result of the selectiveness of our attention to prevent us from getting lost in irrelevant information, we may fail to notice the proper spatial and temporal information. On the one hand, failures of selection in space has been demonstrated in experiments of *change blindness* [70] and *change deafness* [78], where observer does not notice a change in a visual and auditory stimulus, respectively. On the other hand, experiments of *attentional blink* [69] and *repetition blindness* [49] have shown that failures can occur along with time; i.e., when new information (even of small amount) continues to arrive, processing it leads to missing other information.

Attacks can exploit these *spatial* and *temporal* attentional vulnerabilities either reactively or proactively. *Reactive attention attacks* exploit inattention to evade detection and do not attempt to change human attention patterns. For example, many Social Engineering (SE) and phishing attacks result from a lack of attention. We provide a defense framework against reactive attention attacks in Chap. 5. In contrast, *proactive attention attacks* aim to strategically influence human attention patterns. For example, an attacker can generate a large volume of feints and hide real attacks among them to overload human operators, delay their responses, and reduce the accuracy of their judgements. We refer to this new form of attacks as the Informational Denial-of-Service (IDoS) attacks and present a formal description of IDoS attacks, their impacts, and associated defense methods in Chap. 6.

1.2.3.3   Vulnerability of Memory

Relying on networks of neurons in the brain, human memory suffers from restricted capacity, limited speed of information storage and retrieval, forgetting, and memory errors. While digital storage devices share the first two memory vulnerabilities, the latter two are unique to human memory. According to Schacter [68], the latter two belong to the *sins of omission* and *commission*, respectively.

Forgetting is the spontaneous or gradual loss of information already stored in an individual's short- or long-term memory. Unlike a digital storage device, humans cannot 'forget on demand'; i.e., items will linger in memory even then they are no longer needed [66].

Memory errors refer to the wrong recall of information. This can include remembering things that have not happened, giving the wrong source for a memory, or making up things that did not happen. Memory errors are caused in part by the structure of neuron networks as well as a feature of human memorization. As shown in the Deese–Roediger–McDermott paradigm [20], humans incorrectly recall an absent word as it is related to a list of words that belong to a common theme. Many factors (e.g., the degree of attention, motivation, emotional state, and environment where memorization takes place) can affect human memory. For example, the *emotional enhancement of memory* [33] has demonstrated that emotional stimuli are more easily remembered than neutral stimuli.

Human memory vulnerabilities directly lead to security risks. For example, humans use simple and meaningful passwords, reuse the same password over different sites, and even write down the passwords to remember them. These practices make the passwords insecure. As will be introduced in Definition 1.2, cognitive reliability methods, including Single Sign-On (SSO)[2] [62], cognitive passwords [89], and graphical passwords [6], are introduced to mitigate memory vulnerability concerning passwords.

Attackers can also actively exploit those memory vulnerabilities and manipulate the above factors to create attack vectors. For example, attackers can reduce the attack frequency to exploit the forgetting vulnerability. As demonstrated in [67] and [48], lower frequency and likelihood of phishing events increase victim's susceptibility to phishing cyberattacks. Due to the *suggestibility* of human memory (i.e., humans are inclined to accept and act on the suggestions of others), attackers can design phishing emails to trigger memory errors and inject false memories by designing misleading hints. Moreover, they can use emotional language to enhance the operator's false memory and facilitate trust.

---

[2] Single SSO allows a user to log in several related systems with a single ID and password. It reduces the total number of passwords to remember.

1.2.3.4   Vulnerability of Mental Operations

Mental operation vulnerabilities primarily refer to a variety of cognitive biases and exploitable traits. In the history of human development, we have developed cognitive shortcuts and biases for rapid, although less accurate or reasonable, responses to survive in highly dynamic and uncertain environments. However, those cognitive biases expand the *attack surface* and make humans susceptible to SE attacks. We list some of the cognitive biases and the potential adversarial exploitation [64] below.

- **Anchoring**: An individual's decisions are influenced by a particular reference point (i.e., an "anchor"). Pretexting SE can create a situation and initial context to increase the attack's apparent legitimacy and the likelihood of success. Anchoring bias keeps people from questioning the initial impression and accepting the scam.
- **Framing**: An individual can draw different conclusions from the same information, depending on how that information is presented (e.g., as a loss or a gain). Attackers can utilize the framing effect to craft the content of phishing emails and distort human risk perception.
- **Optimism bias**: People tend to have unrealistic optimism; e.g., overestimating the likelihood of positive events and underestimating the likelihood of negative events. Users frequently believe others are more susceptible than they are [18]. Since they think they are immune to attacks, they tend to resist preventive defense measures, including patching, virus scanning, clearing cache, checking for secure sites before entering credit card information, or paying attention to spear phishing.
- **Ingroup bias**: People are social animals and give preferential treatment to in-group members over out-group ones. An attacker can pretend to be affiliated with the group to gain trust and influence the decisions of group members.

In marketing and persuasion, Cialdini [16] deduced six principles of influence from experimental and field studies based on exploitable personal traits. Attackers can also take advantage of the following traits to complete the compromise.

- **Reciprocity**: SE attackers frequently offer victims something to set the stage for reciprocity. For example, people are less likely to refuse an inappropriate request from someone who has provided them with a gift in advance.
- **Social proof**: Individuals are easily influenced by the decisions of a large group of people. An attacker can impersonate the involvement of a victim's friends in order to compel victims to act.
- **Authority**: People tend to conform to authority, and attackers can exploit that by pretending to be a system administrator or a security expert.
- **Liking**: Since it is much easier to influence a person who likes you, attackers can attempt to be likeable by being polite and using concepts, languages, and appearances familiar to the target.

- **Scarcity**: Something in short supply can increase its sense of value. Social engineers may use scarcity (e.g., a limited-time offer) to create a feeling of urgency and spur the victim's action.
- **Commitments and consistency**: Once people make a choice, they receive pressure from others and themselves to adhere to it. SE attacks can induce the victim to make a seemingly insignificant commitment and then escalate the requests. People tend to accept the escalation of commitment as long as the subsequent requests are consistent with the prior commitment.

1.2.4 Cognitive Attack

In Sect. 1.2.3, we discuss four types of exploitable vulnerabilities in the cognitive process. Cognitive attacks refer to the adversarial processes that involve the exploitation of these human vulnerabilities, as defined in Definition 1.1.

Definition 1.1 (Cognitive Attacks) Cognitive attacks are a class of cyber-physical-human processes that manipulate the behaviors of human actors for malicious purposes, including the theft or damage of confidential data and disruption or misdirection of the HCPS services, by exploiting their cognitive vulnerabilities.

Analogous to cyber kill chains,[3] we present the kill chain of cognitive attacks in Sect. 1.2.4.1. Then, in Sect. 1.2.4.2, we zoom into the execution phase of the kill chain and use SE and IDoS attacks as two examples to illustrate the cross-layer attack paths of cognitive attacks.

1.2.4.1 Kill Chain of Cognitive Attacks

Figure 1.5 illustrates the conceptual kill chain of cognitive attacks that consists of six stages in blue arrows. We map the six kill-chain stages into the four attack phases of the attack stack in Fig. 1.3 at the bottom of Fig. 1.5 in orange.

In the reconnaissance phase, the attacker analyzes the information collected from the HCPS. For example, an attacker can formulate the behavioral baseline of a user or an operator during the reconnaissance. Such a baseline can help the attack identify the human vulnerabilities of the target users and exploit them in the execution phase. In the planning phase, the attackers identify the valuable assets and tailor their Tactics, Techniques, and Procedures (TTP) accordingly. We divide the execution phase into three stages. First, attackers exploit human vulnerabilities directly or indirectly, where we show several examples of exploitation paths in Sect. 1.2.4.2. Second, attackers monitor the human target's responses (e.g., emotions

---

[3] An example cyber kill chains developed by Lockheed Martin in 2011 can be found at https://www.lockheedmartin.com/en-us/capabilities/cyber/cyber-kill-chain.html.

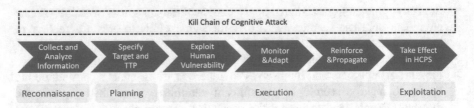

Fig. 1.5 The illustration of the kill chain of cognitive attacks concerning the four-stage attack phases of reconnaissance, planning, execution, and exploitation. In the execution stage, cognitive attacks exploit human vulnerabilities, monitor their responses, and adapt the exploitation TTP accordingly. Then, they choose the best attack setting to reinforce the compromise effect and spread it to a group of victims from the initial victim

and behaviors) and adapt their TTP. For example, attackers can choose to increase or decrease the attack frequency for cautious and careless users, respectively. After the attackers obtain the optimal attack setting, they continue to reinforce the cognitive exploitation and propagate the compromise to other victims related to the initial human target. For example, after gaining trust, attackers can ask the initial victim to forward emails to his colleague, who will become less doubtful about the legitimacy of the phishing emails. In the exploitation phase, cognitive exploitation begins to take effect in human behaviors and subsequently the cyber and physical layers.

1.2.4.2   Example Paths of Cognitive Attacks

Exploiting human vulnerabilities is a critical step in the attack stage of execution. It can take different forms and involve one or many of the cognitive vulnerabilities described in Sect. 1.2.3. In Fig. 1.6, we use SE and IDoS attacks as two examples to illustrate the various forms and procedures of cognitive attacks.

SE attacks directly manipulate the stimulus (e.g., phishing content) and external factors (e.g., peer pressure) to compromise human users. In this type of cognitive attack, cognitive compromise is used as the stepping stone to enter the CPS and perpetrate the technical compromise.

However, in other cognitive attacks, the technical compromise may also serve as a precondition to exploit human cognitive vulnerabilities, as illustrated by the attack path of IDoS attacks. IDoS attacks first generate a lot of feint attacks to trigger cyber alerts that are displayed through a HMI. Human operators investigating these alerts in real-time can suffer from *cognitive overload*, which leads to reduced accuracy and speed in processing the alerts. Since human operators may be unable to respond to alerts associated with the real and significant attacks, these attacks have the potential to disrupt both cyber and physical processes. Examples of real-world IDoS attacks widely exist but are usually implicit in many attack incidents. The following three incidents in Examples 1.2.1, 1.2.2, and 1.2.3 use Distributed Denial-of-Service (DDoS) attacks as a "smoke shell" to attract security analysts' attention while simultaneously launching other stealthy attacks.

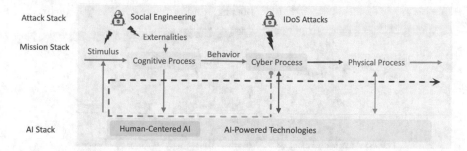

Fig. 1.6 Example paths of cognitive attacks are depicted in the dashed arrow. SE attacks directly exploit human cognitive vulnerabilities by changing stimuli and influencing external factors. IDoS attacks first compromise the cyber process and use technical compromise as a stepping stone to affect the HMI (e.g., by creating feints to increase the operator's cognitive load), which indirectly manipulates the cognitive process. Both types of cognitive attacks have an impact on the cyber and physical processes

Example 1.2.1 (Sony PSN Data Breach 2011) In April 2011, the Security Operation Center (SOC) of Sony was occupied dealing with a DDoS attack, and they overlooked the extraction of confidential information, including the names, addresses, dates of birth, and passwords, of 77 million PlayStation Network (PSN) customers. Authorities in the U.K. fined the Sony company the equivalent of almost $400,000 for the PSN data breach [27].

Example 1.2.2 (BIPS BTC Stolen 2013) Europe's primary bitcoin payment processor for merchants and free online wallet service, BIPS, became the target of a massive DDoS attack on November 15th, 2013. While the SOC was busy to get the system back online, the attacker launched a subsequent attack to gain access and compromise several wallets, resulting in the theft of 1295 BTC (approximately 1 million dollars) [72].

Example 1.2.3 (Tesla Ransomware 2021) A recent thwarted cybersecurity attack against Tesla in 2021 planned to use DDoS attack to divert security analysts' attention from malware that extracted confidential data [74].

1.2.5 Cognitive Security

The development of the AI-powered CPS begins with reliability assurance that the system and AI technologies can remain trustworthy and efficient under uncertainty, disturbances, and failures. The presence of attacks requires us to incorporate defenses, which leads to the concept of security. Analogous to reliability and security in CPS, we define and distinguish cognitive reliability and cognitive security in Definitions 1.2 and 1.3, respectively, forming the four quadrants in Fig. 1.7.

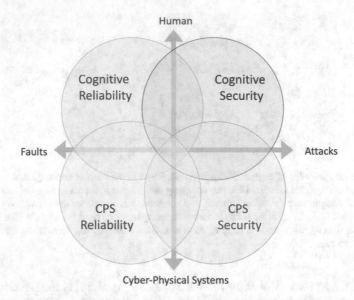

Fig. 1.7 Four quadrants of security and reliability in CPSs and HCPSs. The horizontal arrows distinguish security and reliability based on whether attacks are present or absent, respectively. The vertical arrows distinguish security (or reliability) in HCPSs or CPSs based on whether cognitive vulnerabilities are involved or not. Cognitive security generalizes SE and its mitigation through the additional investigation of the cross-layer impact on HCPSs and the development of human-technical defense technologies to deter the kill chain of cognitive attacks

Definition 1.2 (Cognitive Reliability) Cognitive reliability is the capacity of an HCPS to maintain the continuity of operations, fulfill a designated mission, and provide services at the desired level under stated conditions, including challenging environments of uncertainty, disturbance, and errors.

Definition 1.3 (Cognitive Security) Cognitive security is the practice of deploying people, policies, processes, and technologies to withstand cognitive attacks in Definition 1.1 and defend essential HCPS components, including humans, critical system structures, services, and sensitive information.

1.2.5.1   Cognitive Reliability vs. Cognitive Security

From Definition 1.2, cognitive reliability focuses on Human Reliability Analysis (HRA) and human-centered system design. On the one hand, HRA identifies potential human error events, evaluates the contributing factors, estimates the probability of those errors, and analyzes their impact on the CPS. A variety of methods exist for HRA, including techniques based on probabilistic risk analysis and cognition control, where Di Pasquale et al. [22] refers to these two classes of techniques as the first and second generations of HRA, respectively. These HRA techniques have been widely used in life-critical industrial control systems (e.g., nuclear power plants) to minimize the adverse consequences of human behaviors on the technical systems.

On the other hand, human-centered system design includes ergonomics and behavioral science to understand human cognition processes, adapt the system to human factors to enhance usability, and reduce erroneous behaviors. For example, based on the behavioral science findings that *recognition is significantly easier than recall*, text-based challenge-response mechanisms have been applied in user-to-computer authentication as an improvement over unaided password recall [89]. Other cognitive science results have been used in user authentication and email encryption for usable security [61]; e.g., a graphical password emerges because people memorize pictures better than texts.

Cognitive security in Definition 1.3 is a concept associated with cognitive attacks in Sect. 1.2.4. Unlike human-induced failures in cognitive reliability, cognitive attacks can directly take advantage of cognitive weaknesses and use them as stepping stones to maximize the attack gain. The term "*at the desired level under stated conditions*" in Definition 1.2 indicates that cognitive reliability has a specific goal of system efficiency and usability for a set of defined conditions. Performance under these conditions enables cognitive functions to "*withstand attacks*" or errors up to a certain capacity. For attacks that are beyond such capacity, defense methods are needed to provide further protection, as suggested in Definition 1.3. Protection methods usually come at the cost of reduced efficiency (e.g., false alarms of an Intrusion Detection System (IDS) disrupting normal operation) and usability (e.g., additional effort needed to comply with security procedures). Security designs that aim to augment the capacity needs to takes into account the tradeoff among security, efficiency, and usability in a holistic manner. Such a rationale leads to the system-scientific perspectives, which will be discussed in Sect. 1.3.

1.2.5.2   CIA Triad of Cognitive Security

In the context of cognitive security, we discuss confidentiality, integrity, and availability, i.e., the CIA triad, to provide a guide for the development of theoretical foundations in the ensuing chapters. Confidentiality aims to minimize the leakage of cognitive information and sensitive HCPS data. For example, research has shown that the data leakage from Brain-Computer Interfaces (BCI) can be used to infer personality traits and cognitive abilities [52, 81]. An attacker can impersonate and masquerade as legitimate entities to collect confidential information using phishing attacks. The attacker can use the information to acquire access credentials, steal data, and deploy malware (e.g., Stuxnet [17] and ransomware [85]). When the attacker obtains more sensitive personal information, the impersonation and disguise become more credible, which leads to the compromise of the confidentiality of more victims.

Integrity assesses whether the cognitive process depicted in Fig. 1.4 has been manipulated to induce biased actions. Information and data can be poisoned to manipulate the perception of human operators and users. Even when the information is intact, humans can also be misled into paying attention to the wrong information.

Furthermore, nudging and external influence can mislead human judgment [1, 75]. Examples of cognitive attacks that compromise integrity include misinformation propagation and belief manipulation techniques (e.g., data poisoning [83], gaslighting [84], and fake news [32]).

Cognitive availability plays an important role in monitoring and responding to alerts and disruptions. Cognitive availability attacks can disrupt the cognitive process depicted in Fig. 1.4. Information can be intentionally hidden from humans. Even with uncompromised information, humans can be made oblivious to it in the decision-making process. For example, IDoS attacks compromise the availability of attention by depleting the limited cognitive resources, including attention, memory, and decision-making capacity.

1.2.5.3   Cognitive and Technical Defenses for Cognitive Security

Cognitive security solutions synthesize cognitive and technical defenses to break the kill chain of cognitive attacks, as shown in Fig. 1.8. One part of the defense is cyber and physical, since an essential goal of the cognitive attacks includes technical exploitation across the cyber and physical layers, as shown in the IDoS attack path in Sect. 1.2.4.2.

The other focus of the cognitive security aims to defend humans with educational and AI solutions. User training is one common solution in the corporate world to provide users with security knowledge, raise security awareness, and cultivate

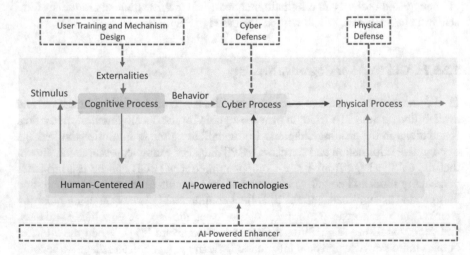

Fig. 1.8 The defense methods in blue dashed boxes aim to break the kill chain of cognitive attacks and improve the cognitive security. The cyber and physical defenses take effect on the cyber and physical processes, respectively. User training and human-centered mechanism design affect the cognitive process through externalities. Incorporating the AI stack, cognitive security includes the AI-powered enhancer to protect HCPSs from the adversarial exploitation of AI technologies

critical thinking, which consolidates the cognitive process. The training may take a long time to take effect and may not be reliable after a period of time. We can augment this educational solution with other schemes enabled by AI technologies, including alert systems to detect misbehavior and incentive mechanisms to elicit behaviors that are conducive to network security [8, 9, 37].

AI-technologies in the AI stack can also be susceptible to cognitive attacks. It is essential for the AI-powered enhancer to guarantee the security and resilience of the AI-powered technologies. In particular, human-centered AI technologies in the AI stack need to not only tilt the cognitive biases when augmenting human capacities but also be aware of and defend against cognitive attacks. For example, AI-enabled security assistive technologies can augment HMI to defend against the threat of IDoS attacks, as we will elaborate on in Chap. 6. To this end, we fuse various biosensor data, including optical, motion, acoustic signals, and electrical biosignals, to capture the cognitive state in real time.[4] These signals can be fed back to the AI-enhancer for adaptive control.

We can analogize the human process augmented by AI-powered technologies in Fig. 1.8 as the learning process of children under the supervision of their parents. While user training and auxiliary schemes teach and motivate children to behave securely, these methods are subject to social and cognitive limitations. The AI-powered enhancer plays a supervisory role, providing situational awareness and protecting against potential attacks on humans.

1.2.5.4 Scope of Cognitive Security

Cognitive security is a research topic in its infancy. We elaborate the characteristics of cognitive security defined in Definition 1.3 using the running examples of SE and IDoS attacks.

First, the exploitation of the vulnerabilities of human cognition distinguishes cognitive security from the realm of CPS security. The area explores cognition-related attack models and their associated defense mechanisms. It is clear that cognitive vulnerabilities enlarge the *attack surface* of the CPS. It will lead to a new class of *HCPS attacks* that leverage cognitive exploitation as a critical step or component.

Second, in connection with HCPS, cognitive security extends the scope of SE and *cognitive hacking* [19]. On top of the cognitive manipulation in human-human interactions, we further investigate its impacts and dependency on the human-machine interaction in HCPS. As illustrated in the IDoS example, cyber-physical exploitation can build on the attentional vulnerability to exacerbate its impact on the HCPS. Such *human-technical attacks* that directly exploit human cognition limitations are beyond the scope of SE and cognitive hacking.

---

[4] Studies such as [15, 50, 63] provide more information about combination of biosignals for cognitive state estimation and monitoring.

Third, the goal of cognitive security in this book is not to augment humans' inherent cognition capabilities through innovations at the scientific frontier of neuroscience or biomedical sciences, such as medications or medical therapies. Instead, we focus on designing non-intrusive mechanisms and assistive technologies to influence and affect human cognitive processes, change their behaviors, and ultimately enhance the security of the entire HCPS.

Fourth, there are many open research questions in cognitive security. For example, *what leads to inattentional blindness? How to create credible misinformation and persuasive messages? How to design anti-phishing interfaces?* The focus of this book is to address research questions at the *system level*. The approach distinguishes itself from those that create domain-specific knowledge in, e.g., cognitive sciences and human psychology. Instead, it develops *input-output* system models that build on the theories and empirical findings from behavioral science and psychology. By integrating the system-level models, it creates a holistic human-cyber-physical framework. As one example, we will demonstrate in Chap. 5 how we create a data-driven, system-scientific approach to designing the optimal anti-phishing interface.

Fifth, the defense against cognitive threats relies on either human or technical solutions. Human solutions include training and education, while technical ones create assistive AI technologies. A technical defense solution needs to be aware of and adapt to adverse exploitation of cognitive vulnerabilities. For example, as we will demonstrate in Chap. 6, under the threat of IDoS attacks, it may be insufficient to adopt the traditional method of alert triage to indirectly reduce cognitive load. Therefore, we further de-emphasize alerts strategically to manage attention and make the alert inspection process compatible with each operator's cognitive load.

Sixth, cognitive defense is essential but not a necessity. On the one hand, we may not need to defend against all types of cognitive attacks, as it is sufficient to break the kill chain of attacks that exploit cognitive vulnerabilities. For example, by eliminating the exploitation stage of the attack kill chain in Fig. 1.5, we can safeguard the HCPS system even if humans are misled to make cognitive errors in the execution stage. Cognitive resilience, on the other hand, is a complementary concept to maintain the function of the HCPS despite the limited cognitive defense. Since many types of cognitive attacks are challenging or too costly, if not impossible, to defend against, perfect security is not always permissible. Resilient mechanisms will be the next reasonable goal of protection to reduce the risk and impact of the attacks.

Finally, cognitive security in this book does not aim to increase human cognitive capacities (e.g., cognitive computing SOC [21], phishing detector [28], and incident management systems [2]). Other topics that are beyond the scope of this book include the use of human cognitive strengths (e.g., the creativity and flexibility of human cognition, discussed in Chap. 3) to augment technical defense systems, and the improvement of the usability of the security measures [29, 61]. They contribute to other essential dimensions of cognitive security.

1.3   System-Scientific Perspectives for Cognitive Security

Humans are an essential component in accomplishing CPS missions, and cognitive security needs to incorporate rather than eschew human cognition. Human cognition, however, is of high complexity, uncertainty, and individual difference, which leads to the following research questions:

- *How to incorporate established theories of human factors into HCPSs for defensive purposes?*
- *How to customize the defense and make it adaptive to various security applications?*
- *What are useful metrics and measures to quantify the impact of human factors on a CPS and the effectiveness of the defense methods?*

This book adopts a system-scientific perspective, incorporating decision theory, optimization, game theory, AI, physiological metrics, and psychology theories (as illustrated at the right bottom of Fig. 1.1) to address these questions for the following reasons.

- First, as illustrated in Sect. 1.2.4, cognitive attacks occur at the *cognition level* (e.g., SE) and the *system level* (e.g., IDoS attacks) rather than the *neuronal level*. Thus, the attack and defense interactions also need to be investigated at the cognition and system levels to understand the entire attack phase, anticipate the interaction of attacks with the HCPS, and find defensible points among these phases.
- Second, cognitive attacks (e.g., IDoS attacks) exploit distinct vulnerabilities in human, cyber, and physical processes. A single tool is not sufficient to deter, detect, and prevent these cross-layer, cross-disciplinary attacks. To safeguard diverse vulnerabilities, we need interdisciplinary tools to synthesize defense methods from multiple areas.
- Third, since cognitive attacks have an impact on human, cyber, and physical processes, it is important to quantify the risk for each component, the propagation of the risk, and the risk to the entire HCPS [13, 39, 40]. Moreover, we need to design optimal controllables to defend HCPSs cost-effectively. Therefore, we need scientific and quantitative approaches to quantify security metrics and bounds, assess tradeoffs, characterize fundamental limits, and design optimal control [57, 80, 82].
- Fourth, since both cognitive attackers and defenders are intelligent players, they take actions based on the predictions of the others. Game theory becomes a natural tool to capture the interactions in an adversarial environment for quantitative analysis and design [43, 55, 86, 87].
- Fifth, models may not accurately describe HCPS components (e.g., human cognition) that are highly dynamic and sometimes unobservable. Data collected by biosensors (e.g., electroencephalogram (EEG) and eye-tracking devices) and AI can be incorporated to provide system-level adaptive solutions in response to the measurable observations.

- Finally, theories from psychology and social science can be adopted to understand sensation, attention, memory, and decisions. As a multi-disciplinary method, a system-scientific approach incorporates those findings and results to create holistic data-driven and model-based system frameworks of HCPSs.

1.3.1 Advantages of System-Scientific Approaches

System-scientific approaches provide a new paradigm for cognitive security and enable the following advantages.

- **Emergence and Enabling Discoveries**: The emergence of new phenomena and discoveries commonly arises in philosophy, psychology, and the arts in scenarios where "the whole is something else than the sum of its parts" [51].[5] As shown in Fig. 1.2, the close integration of AI and humans in CPSs leads to the new concept of HCPSs. The interactions among human, cyber, physical, and AI components create new attack surfaces and attack paths, which potentially amplifies the human cognitive vulnerabilities and promotes the need for research in the emerging field of cognitive security. The study of complex HCPSs requires interdisciplinary methods to create relevant models of appropriate resolutions and scales. Recent efforts have developed system methods such as games-in-games [12, 85, 86], factored games [38, 41], and spatio-temporal attack graphs [34] to abstract different system characteristics and understand essential performances in adversarial environments. The integration of cognitive science methods with CPSs will necessitate the use and development of sophisticated system-scientific tools to bridge the multiple areas.
- **Black Box and Function Simulation**: A system perspective focuses on the input and output (or the transfer characteristics) of the system, where the system itself is treated as a black box without any knowledge of its internal workings. By treating human cognition systems as black boxes, we focus on the *behavior-level impact* rather than the *cognitive- or neuro-level mechanisms* that can be complicated and not well-understood. The input-output view also enables us to simulate a system's function without establishing the internal model of the system. This view has proven successful in economic modeling [53, 73], system biology [45, 88], and drug delivery systems [60, 79].
- **Modular and Multi-Scale Design**: A system can be represented by its constituent subsystems, which are described by multi-scale function-relevant system models. For example, the HCPS system consists of human, cyber, and physical subsystems. The human subsystem further contains cognition systems consisting of sensation, attention, memory, and mental operations. Depending on the purpose of the model, we can zoom into the proper level of subsystem. Since

---

[5] The definition is often misquoted as 'the whole is greater than the sum of its parts'.

these subsystems interact through their inputs and outputs, there is flexibility to amend and update each subsystem. It leads to a modular design, which has played an important role in system resilience. For example, games-in-games principles presented in [86] aim to create zoom-in and zoom-out system optimization techniques for complex cyber-physical systems. Ref. [11] has leveraged a bottom-up game-theoretic approach to design optimal and resilient generation policies for distributed renewable resources and their integration into the power grid. Ref. [14] has discussed the goal of achieving mosaic command and control and leveraging system and control methods to achieve flexible multi-agent teaming in multi-domain battlefields.

- **Quantitative Strategies and Optimization**: The system-scientific models enable a quantitative description of the situation and the formulation of optimal design problems that lead to cost-effective security mechanisms. The integration of multiple system-scientific approaches, including deterministic and stochastic methods, data-driven and model-based tools, and static and dynamic frameworks, gives rise to an appropriate level of abstraction of function-relevant models that can address the design question. For example, the design of cognition-aware control systems would need to zoom into the control system while zooming out the cognitive system and connecting them through relevant input-output relationships. Similarly, the control-aware incentive mechanism would zoom into the decision-making processes of the cognitive system and zoom out the other components of the cognitive processes while interacting with relevant control system models.

1.4 Outline and Organization

The rest of the book is organized as follows. Chapter 2 provides an overview of the essential system-scientific tools in modeling, analyzing, and mitigating cognitive vulnerabilities. The chapter overviews decision theory, game theory, and reinforcement learning to provide a background for later chapters. Chapter 3 discusses in further detail situation awareness, decision-making, and collaborations as three indispensable classes of human cognitive capacities in designing, operating, supervising, and securing an HCPS. As a double-edged sword, the active presence of human cognition in an HCPS also brings innate and acquired cognitive vulnerabilities based on whether they can be mitigated through short-term external interference. Chapter 4 provides a review of system-scientific perspectives to characterize the vulnerability, the attacks, and the defense methods in different HCPS security scenarios. Two system-scientific models, ADVERT [44] and RADAMS [35, 36], are presented in Chaps. 5 and 6 to defend against phishing and IDoS attacks that exploit attention vulnerabilities reactively and proactively, respectively. Both system-scientific models create human-technical solutions by utilizing human data and Reinforcement Learning (RL) for adaptive strategies. We conclude the book in

Chap. 7 and discuss future directions to expand the breadth, abundance, and depth of cognitive security.

References

1. Akerlof GA, Shiller RJ (2015) Phishing for phools. Princeton University Press, Princeton
2. Andrade R, Torres J, Cadena S (2019) Cognitive security for incident management process. In: International conference on information technology & systems. Springer, Berlin, pp 612–621
3. Arons B (1992) A review of the cocktail party effect. J Am Voice I/O Soc 12(7):35–50
4. Barmer H, Dzombak R, Gaston M, Palat V, Redner F, Smith T, et al (2021) Scalable AI. Tech. rep., Carnegie Mellon University. https://doi.org/10.1184/R1/16560273.v1
5. Bereiter-Hahn J, Strohmeier R, Kunzenbacher I, Beck K, Voth M (1981) Locomotion of xenopus epidermis cells in primary culture. J Cell Sci 52(1):289–311
6. Biddle R, Chiasson S, Van Oorschot PC (2012) Graphical passwords: learning from the first twelve years. ACM Comput Surv 44(4):1–41
7. Bruce V, Green PR, Georgeson MA (2003) Visual perception: physiology, psychology, & ecology. Psychology Press, Hove
8. Casey WA, Zhu Q, Morales JA, Mishra B (2015) Compliance control: managed vulnerability surface in social-technological systems via signaling games. In: Proceedings of the 7th ACM CCS international workshop on managing insider security threats, pp 53–62
9. Casey W, Morales JA, Wright E, Zhu Q, Mishra B (2016) Compliance signaling games: toward modeling the deterrence of insider threats. Comput Math Organ Theory 22(3):318–349
10. Chaczko Z, Kulbacki M, Gudzbeler G, Alsawwaf M, Thai-Chyzhykau I, Wajs-Chaczko P (2020) Exploration of explainable AI in context of human-machine interface for the assistive driving system. In: Asian conference on intelligent information and database systems. Springer, Berlin, pp 507–516
11. Chen J, Zhu Q (2016) A game-theoretic framework for resilient and distributed generation control of renewable energies in microgrids. IEEE Trans Smart Grid 8(1):285–295
12. Chen J, Zhu Q (2019) Control of multilayer mobile autonomous systems in adversarial environments: a games-in-games approach. IEEE Trans Control Netw Syst 7(3):1056–1068
13. Chen J, Zhu Q (2019) A game-and decision-theoretic approach to resilient interdependent network analysis and design. Springer, Berlin
14. Chen J, Zhu Q (2019) A games-in-games approach to mosaic command and control design of dynamic network-of-networks for secure and resilient multi-domain operations. In: Sensors and systems for space applications XII, SPIE, vol 11017, pp 189–195
15. Chen X, Li Y, Wang Z, Zhang J (2018) Real-time cognitive state monitoring using a combination of physiological sensors. IEEE Trans Biomed Eng 65(4):913–922
16. Cialdini RB (2007) Influence: the psychology of persuasion, vol 55. Collins, New York
17. Clark A, Zhu Q, Poovendran R, Başar T (2013) An impact-aware defense against Stuxnet. In: 2013 American control conference. IEEE, pp 4140–4147
18. Cox EB, Zhu Q, Balcetis E (2020) Stuck on a phishing lure: differential use of base rates in self and social judgments of susceptibility to cyber risk. Compr Results Soc Psychol 4(1):25–52
19. Cybenko G, Giani A, Thompson P (2002) Cognitive hacking: a battle for the mind. Computer 35(8):50–56
20. Deese J (1959) On the prediction of occurrence of particular verbal intrusions in immediate recall. J Exp Psychol 58(1):17
21. Demertzis K, Kikiras P, Tziritas N, Sanchez SL, Iliadis L (2018) The next generation cognitive security operations center: network flow forensics using cybersecurity intelligence. Big Data Cogn Comput 2(4):35

22. Di Pasquale V, Iannone R, Miranda S, Riemma S (2013) An overview of human reliability analysis techniques in manufacturing operations. Oper Manag 221–240

23. Directorate-General for Research and Innovation (European Commission), Breque M, De Nul L, Petridis A (2021) Industry 5.0: towards a sustainable, human-centric and resilient European industry. Publications Office. https://doi.org/10.2777/308407

24. Doghri W, Saddoud A, Chaari Fourati L (2022) Cyber-physical systems for structural health monitoring: sensing technologies and intelligent computing. J Supercomput 78(1):766–809

25. Elgendi M, Kumar P, Barbic S, Howard N, Abbott D, Cichocki A (2018) Subliminal priming—state of the art and future perspectives. Behav Sci 8(6):54

26. Ewen K (1983) Somatic radiation risk in roentgen-diagnosis. Strahlentherapie 159(12):765–771

27. Fisher D (2013) Sony fined £250,000 by UK over failures in playstation network breach. https://threatpost.com/sony-fincd-250000-uk-over-failures-playstation-network-breach-012413/77446/

28. Garcés IO, Cazares MF, Andrade RO (2019) Detection of phishing attacks with machine learning techniques in cognitive security architecture. In: 2019 International conference on Computational Science and Computational Intelligence (CSCI). IEEE, pp 366–370

29. Greenstadt R, Beal J (2008) Cognitive security for personal devices. In: Proceedings of the 1st ACM workshop on AISec, pp 27–30

30. Griffor ER, Greer C, Wollman DA, Burns MJ, et al (2017) Framework for cyber-physical systems: Volume 1, Overview (NIST Special Publication 1500–201). National Institute of Standards and Technology

31. Groshev M, Guimarães C, Martín-Pérez J, de la Oliva A (2021) Toward intelligent cyber-physical systems: digital twin meets artificial intelligence. IEEE Commun Mag 59(8):14–20

32. Guo B, Ding Y, Sun Y, Ma S, Li K, Yu Z (2021) The mass, fake news, and cognition security. Front Comput Sci 15(3):1–13

33. Hamann S (2001) Cognitive and neural mechanisms of emotional memory. Trends Cogn Sci 5(9):394–400

34. Huang L, Zhu Q (2020) Farsighted risk mitigation of lateral movement using dynamic cognitive honeypots. In: International conference on decision and game theory for security. Springer, Cham, pp 125–146

35. Huang L, Zhu Q (2021) Combating informational denial-of-service (IDoS) attacks: modeling and mitigation of attentional human vulnerability. In: International conference on decision and game theory for security. Springer, Cham, pp 314–333

36. Huang L, Zhu Q (2022) Radams: resilient and adaptive alert and attention management strategy against informational denial-of-service (IDoS) attacks. Comput Secur 121:102844

37. Huang L, Zhu Q (2022) Zetar: modeling and computational design of strategic and adaptive compliance policies. arXiv preprint arXiv:220402294. https://doi.org/10.48550/ARXIV.2204.02294

38. Huang L, Chen J, Zhu Q (2017) A factored MDP approach to optimal mechanism design for resilient large-scale interdependent critical infrastructures. In: 2017 workshop on Modeling and Simulation of Cyber-Physical Energy Systems (MSCPES). IEEE, pp 1–6

39. Huang L, Chen J, Zhu Q (2017) A large-scale Markov game approach to dynamic protection of interdependent infrastructure networks. In: International conference on decision and game theory for security. Springer, Berlin, pp 357–376

40. Huang L, Chen J, Zhu Q (2018) Distributed and optimal resilient planning of large-scale interdependent critical infrastructures. In: 2018 Winter Simulation Conference (WSC). IEEE, pp 1096–1107

41. Huang L, Chen J, Zhu Q (2018) Factored Markov game theory for secure interdependent infrastructure networks. In: Game theory for security and risk management. Birkhäuser, Cham, pp 99–126

42. Huang W, Chen X, Jin R, Lau N (2020) Detecting cognitive hacking in visual inspection with physiological measurements. Appl Ergon 84:103022

43. Huang Y, Chen J, Huang L, Zhu Q (2020) Dynamic games for secure and resilient control system design. Natl Sci Rev 7(7):1125–1141
44. Huang L, Jia S, Balcetis E, Zhu Q (2022) Advert: an adaptive and data-driven attention enhancement mechanism for phishing prevention. IEEE Trans Inf Forensics Secur 17:2585–2597
45. Ingalls BP (2013) Mathematical modeling in systems biology: an introduction. MIT Press, Cambridge
46. Johnston WA, Dark VJ (1986) Selective attention. Annu Rev Psychol 37:43–75
47. Jyothsna V, Prasad R, Prasad KM (2011) A review of anomaly based intrusion detection systems. Int J Comput Appl 28(7):26–35
48. Kaivanto K (2014) The effect of decentralized behavioral decision making on system-level risk. Risk Anal 34(12):2121–2142
49. Kanwisher NG (1987) Repetition blindness: type recognition without token individuation. Cognition 27(2):117–143
50. Kim J, Lee J, Park S, Yoon H (2017) A real-time cognitive state monitoring system based on multimodal biosignals. IEEE J Biomed Health Inf 21(5):1346–1354
51. Koffka K (2013) Principles of Gestalt psychology. Routledge, London
52. Landau O, Cohen A, Gordon S, Nissim N (2020) Mind your privacy: privacy leakage through BCI applications using machine learning methods. Knowl-Based Syst 198:105932
53. Leontief W (1986) Input-output economics. Oxford University Press, New York
54. Lindsay GW (2020) Attention in psychology, neuroscience, and machine learning. Front Comput Neurosci 14:29
55. Manshaei MH, Zhu Q, Alpcan T, Başar T, Hubaux JP (2013) Game theory meets network security and privacy. ACM Comput Surv 45(3):1–39
56. Marot A, Rozier A, Dussartre M, Crochepierre L, Donnot B (2022) Towards an AI assistant for power grid operators. HHAI2022: Augmenting Human Intellect. https://doi.org/10.3233/faia22019
57. Meadows DH (2008) Thinking in systems: a primer. Chelsea Green Publishing, Chelsea
58. Molden DC (2014) Understanding priming effects in social psychology. Guilford Publications, New York
59. Pan SJ, Yang Q (2009) A survey on transfer learning. IEEE Trans Knowl Data Eng 22(10):1345–1359
60. Parker RS, Doyle III FJ (2001) Control-relevant modeling in drug delivery. Adv Drug Deliv Rev 48(2–3):211–228
61. Payne BD, Edwards WK (2008) A brief introduction to usable security. IEEE Internet Comput 12(3):13–21
62. Radha V, Reddy DH (2012) A survey on single sign-on techniques. Procedia Technol 4:134–139
63. Raza ST, Alghazzawi D, Imran M, Hasan T (2016) Real-time assessment of cognitive workload in a driving simulator using physiological signals. IEEE Trans Hum Mach Syst 46(2):228–237
64. Rohleder K (2019) Cognitive biases as vulnerabilities. https://www.linkedin.com/pulse/cognitive-biases-vulnerabilities-krinken-rohleder/
65. Salau B, Rawal A, Rawat DB (2022) Recent advances in artificial intelligence for wireless internet of things and cyber-physical systems: a comprehensive survey. IEEE Internet Things J 9:12916–12930
66. Sasse MA, Brostoff S, Weirich D (2001) Transforming the 'weakest link'—a human/computer interaction approach to usable and effective security. BT Technol J 19(3):122–131
67. Sawyer BD, Hancock PA (2018) Hacking the human: the prevalence paradox in cybersecurity. Hum Factors 60(5):597–609
68. Schacter DL (2002) The seven sins of memory: how the mind forgets and remembers. Houghton Mifflin, Boston
69. Shapiro KL, Raymond JE, Arnell KM (1997) The attentional blink. Trends Cogn Sci 1(8):291–296

70. Simons DJ, Rensink RA (2005) Change blindness: past, present, and future. Trends Cogn Sci 9(1):16–20
71. Song J, Lyu D, Zhang Z, Wang Z, Zhang T, Ma L (2022) When cyber-physical systems meet ai: a benchmark, an evaluation, and a way forward. In: ICSE 2022 SEIP
72. Southurst J (2013) Bitcoin payment processor BIPS attacked, over $1 million stolen. https://www.coindesk.com/markets/2013/11/25/bitcoin-payment-processor-bips-attacked-over-1-million-stolen/
73. Tanwani A, Zhu Q (2019) Feedback Nash equilibrium for randomly switching differential–algebraic games. IEEE Trans Autom Control 65(8):3286–3301
74. Team SN (2021) Russian national pleads guilty after trying to hack a human at Tesla. https://www.secureworld.io/industry-news/tesla-hacker-charges-arrested
75. Thaler RH, Sunstein CR (2009) Nudge: improving decisions about health, wealth, and happiness. Penguin, London
76. Tipper SP (1985) The negative priming effect: inhibitory priming by ignored objects. Q J Exp Psychol 37(4):571–590
77. Torabi M, Udzir NI, Abdullah MT, Yaakob R (2021) A review on feature selection and ensemble techniques for intrusion detection system. Int J Adv Comput Sci Appl 12(5):538–553. https://doi.org/10.14569/ijacsa.2021.0120566
78. Vitevitch MS (2003) Change deafness: the inability to detect changes between two voices. J Exp Psychol Hum Percept Perform 29(2):333
79. Voss GI, Katona PG, Chizeck HJ (1987) Adaptive multivariable drug delivery: control of arterial pressure and cardiac output in anesthetized dogs. IEEE Trans Biomed Eng 34(8):617–623
80. Wiener N (2019) Cybernetics or control and communication in the animal and the machine. MIT Press, Cambridge
81. Xia K, Duch W, Sun Y, Xu K, Fang W, Luo H, Zhang Y, Sang D, Xu X, Wang FY, Wu D (2022) Privacy-preserving brain–computer interfaces: a systematic review. IEEE Trans Comput Soc Syst 1–13. https://doi.org/10.1109/tcss.2022.3184818
82. Xu Z, Zhu Q (2016) Cross-layer secure cyber-physical control system design for networked 3d printers. In: 2016 American Control Conference (ACC). IEEE, pp 1191–1196
83. Zhang R, Zhu Q (2017) A game-theoretic defense against data poisoning attacks in distributed support vector machines. In: 2017 IEEE 56th Annual Conference on Decision and Control (CDC). IEEE, pp 4582–4587
84. Zhang Z, Zhu Q (2020) Deceptive kernel function on observations of discrete POMDP. arXiv preprint arXiv:200805585
85. Zhao Y, Ge Y, Zhu Q (2021) Combating ransomware in internet of things: a games-in-games approach for cross-layer cyber defense and security investment. In: International conference on decision and game theory for security. Springer, Berlin, pp 208–228
86. Zhu Q, Basar T (2015) Game-theoretic methods for robustness, security, and resilience of cyberphysical control systems: games-in-games principle for optimal cross-layer resilient control systems. IEEE Control Syst Mag 35(1):46–65
87. Zhu Q, Rass S (2018) Game theory meets network security: a tutorial. In: Proceedings of the 2018 ACM SIGSAC conference on computer and communications security, pp 2163–2165
88. Zhu Q, Tembine H, Başar T (2011) Hybrid risk-sensitive mean-field stochastic differential games with application to molecular biology. In: 2011 50th IEEE conference on decision and control and European control conference. IEEE, pp 4491–4497
89. Zviran M, Haga WJ (1990) Cognitive passwords: the key to easy access control. Comput Secur 9(8):723–736

Chapter 2
System-Scientific Methods

Abstract In Chap. 2, we briefly introduce essential system-scientific tools for modeling, analyzing, and mitigating cognitive vulnerabilities and cognitive attacks. Decision theory in Sect. 2.1 provides a scientific foundation of making decisions for single agents with different rationality levels under stochastic environments. Game theory is introduced in Sect. 2.2 to model the strategic interactions among multiple agents under several basic game settings and their associated Nash Equilibrium (NE) solution concepts. To address the challenges of incomplete information in decision-making and game modeling, we present two learning schemes in Sect. 2.3. These tools provide a system-scientific perspective to evaluate and reduce uncertainty in HCPSs, as illustrated by the blue and red lines in Fig. 2.1, respectively. We refer the readers to the notes at the end of each section for recent advances and relevant references.

Keywords Expected utility theory · Von Neumann–Morgenstern utility theorem · Cumulative prospect theory · Game theory · Nash equilibrium · Bayesian learning · Reinforcement learning

2.1 Decision Theory

A wide range of events are considered stochastic in HCPSs, including the component failure of nuclear power plants and the successful compromise of cyber attacks. For each event, the same behavior can lead to different probabilistic consequences, where the consequence-probability pair is referred to as a "prospect" defined below.

Definition 2.1 (Prospect) Let $X = \{x_1, x_2, \cdots, x_n\}$ represent a mutually exclusive and exhaustive set of $n \in \mathbb{Z}^+$ consequences and p_i represent the probability of $x_i, i \in \{1, 2, \cdots, n\}$, where $p_i \geq 0$ and $\sum_{i=1}^{n} p_i = 1$. A prospect $P := (x_1, p_1; x_2, p_2; \cdots; x_n, p_n)$ is the set of consequence-probability pairs.

We illustrate the concept of prospects with the following defense investment example.

Fig. 2.1 The overall
structure of Chap. 2
concerning uncertainty
evaluation and learning in
blue and red, respectively.
Section 2.1.1 provides a basic
uncertainty evaluation
method, while Sects. 2.1.2
and 2.2 further incorporate
subjectivity and multi-agent
interaction into the
evaluation. Bayesian and
reinforcement learning
schemes in Sects. 2.3.1 and
2.3.2 reduce uncertainty
through external probabilistic
observation and dynamic
interactions, respectively

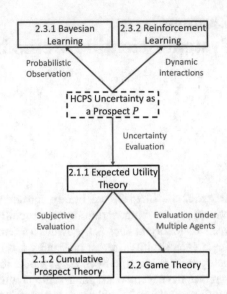

Example 2.1.1 (Defense Investment) Security Operation Center (SOC) needs to
determine whether to adopt a defense method against an attack. Consider a binary
consequence set $X = \{x_S, x_N\}$, where x_S and x_N denote whether the attack is
successful or not, respectively. The attack succeeds with probability p_A and p_N
if the defense method is used or not, respectively. Then, the decision whether to
adopt the defense or not leads to the prospects $P = (x_S, p_A; x_N, 1 - p_A)$ and
$P' = (x_S, p_N; x_N, 1 - p_N)$, respectively.   □

In a stochastic environment, different behaviors lead to different prospects.
Decision theories explain how decision makers compare these prospects and
make decisions. In particular, Expected Utility Theory (EUT) in Sect. 2.1.1 and
Cumulative Prospect Theory (CPT) in Sect. 2.1.2 consider perfectly and boundedly
rational decision-makers, respectively. The structure of Sect. 2.1 is illustrated in
Fig. 2.1.

2.1.1 Expected Utility Theory

Let utility function

$$u : X \mapsto \mathbb{R} \tag{2.1}$$

map from the consequence set to real numbers, where $u(x_i)$ represents the decision
maker's evaluation of the consequence $x_i, i \in \{1, \cdots, n\}$. In Expected Utility

Theory (EUT), a decision-maker chooses an action that maximizes the expected utility defined as

$$\mathbb{E}(P) := \sum_{i=1}^{n} u(x_i) p_i. \tag{2.2}$$

We continue the discussion of defense investment in Example 2.1.1 as follows to illustrate EUT.

Example 2.1.2 (Defense Investment Cont.) Suppose that the defense method has a cost of c and the successful attack brings a monetary loss of l. Then, the utility function $u(x_S) = -l - c, u(x_N) = -c$ (resp. $u(x_S) = -l, u(x_N) = 0$) if the defense method is (resp. not) applied. According to (2.2), we have $\mathbb{E}(P) = (-l - c)p_A + (-c)(1 - p_A)$ and $\mathbb{E}(P') = (-l)p_N + (0)(1 - p_N)$. EUT predicts that the defender chooses to adopt the defense if $\mathbb{E}(P) \geq \mathbb{E}(P')$. □

Although Bernoulli [4] proposed the aforementioned expected utility hypothesis in 1738, it was not until the development of the Von Neumann–Morgenstern (VNM) utility theorem [27] in 1947 that laid the theoretical foundation of EUT. The VNM theorem shown in Theorem 2.1 is based on the following four axioms under the notation of preference in Definition 2.2.

Definition 2.2 (Preference) If a decision maker prefers prospect P over prospect P', we write $P \succ P'$, or equivalently, $P' \prec P$. If the agent is indifferent between P and P', we write $P \sim P'$. If P is either preferred over or viewed with indifference relative to P', we write $P \succeq P'$, or equivalently, $P' \preceq P$.

Axiom 1 (Completeness) For any prospects P, P', exactly one of the following holds: $P \succ P', P \prec P'$, or $P \sim P'$.

Axiom 2 (Transitivity) If $P \preceq P'$ and $P' \preceq P''$, then $P \preceq P''$.

Axiom 3 (Continuity) If $P \preceq P' \preceq P''$, then there exists probability $p_0 \in [0, 1]$ such that $p_0 P + (1 - p_0) P'' \sim P'$, where the notation on the left side refers to a situation in which P is received with probability p_0 and P'' is received with probability $1 - p_0$.

Axiom 4 (Independence) For any prospect P'' and probability $p_0 \in [0, 1]$, $P \preceq P'$ if and only if $p_0 P + (1 - p_0) P'' \preceq p_0 P' + (1 - p_0) P''$.

Theorem 2.1 (VNM Utility Theorem [27]) *For any VNM-rational agent (i.e., satisfying Axioms 1–4), there exists a utility function u defined in (2.1) such that for any two prospects P, P' defined in Definition 2.1,*

$$P \prec P' \quad \textit{if and only if} \quad \mathbb{E}(u(P)) < \mathbb{E}(u(P')), \tag{2.3}$$

where expectation $\mathbb{E}$ is defined in (2.2).

2.1.2 Cumulative Prospect Theory

EUT in Sect. 2.1.1 provides a reasonable benchmark to compare between prospects and make decisions. However, human behaviors are not always rational and can violate the axioms. Tversky and Kahneman develop Cumulative Prospect Theory (CPT) [19] based on the following three observations:

- **Framing Effect**: People use a certain reference point, denoted by $r_0 \in \mathbb{R}$, to judge the possible outcomes. For a given consequence $x_i, i \in \{1, \cdots, n\}$, the relative value compared to the reference point (i.e., $u(x_i) - r_0$) matters more than the absolute value $u(x_i)$.
- **Loss Aversion**: Humans prefer avoiding losses to acquiring equivalent gains.
- **Extreme Overweight**: People tend to overweigh extreme events but underweigh "average" events.

To incorporate the first two observations, CPT introduces a pair of value functions $v_+^\gamma : \mathbb{R}^{+,0} \mapsto \mathbb{R}^{0,+}$ and $v_-^{\gamma,\lambda} : \mathbb{R}^- \mapsto \mathbb{R}^{0,+}$ that distort the relative utility function according to the human subject evaluation. The value function is usually in an asymmetric "S" shape and steeper for losses than gains due to loss aversion. Figure 2.2a illustrates a classical value function, where a larger $\lambda > 0$ represents a high level of loss aversion, and a larger γ represents a higher diminishing sensitivity. CPT incorporates the third observation by introducing a distortion w on the Cumulative Distribution Function (CDF). Figure 2.2b illustrates a classical "S"-shape distortion, where a larger $\beta > 0$ represents a high level of extreme overweight.

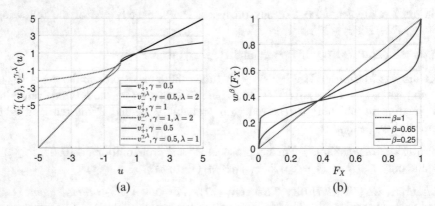

Fig. 2.2 CPT distorts the utility function and CDF to incorporate the observations of framing effect, loss aversion, and extreme overweight. (a) Value functions $v_+^\gamma(u) = (u - r_0)^\gamma, u \geq r_0$; $v_-^{\gamma,\lambda}(u) = -\lambda(-(u - r_0))^\gamma, u < r_0$. (b) Probability weighting function $w^\beta(F_X) = \exp(-(-\log(F_X))^\beta)$ on CDF F_X.

Table 2.1 Reordering of positive relative utilities

	x_4	x_2	
Relative gain value	$40 - r_0$	$20 - r_0$	
Probability	1/8	1/4	
CDF F_X	0	1/8	3/8

Table 2.2 Reordering of negative relative utilities

	x_5	x_3	x_1	
Relative loss value	$-50 - r_0$	$-30 - r_0$	$-10 - r_0$	
Probability	1/8	1/3	1/6	
CDF F_X	0	1/8	11/24	5/8

Under CPT, decision makers choose an action that maximizes the revised expected utility denoted by $\mathbb{E}_{CPT}$. We use the following example to illustrate how $\mathbb{E}_{CPT}$ is obtained.

Example 2.1.3 (CPT Computation) Consider a prospect $P = (x_1, 1/6; x_2, 1/8; x_3, 1/3; x_4, 1/4; x_5, 1/8)$ and a reference point $r_0 = 10$. Let $u(x_i) = (-1)^i \times 10 \times i, i \in \{1, 2, \cdots, 5\}$. First, we reorder the positive and negative relative utilities $u(x_i) - r_0$ under $x_i, i \in \{1, 2, \cdots, 5\}$, in Tables 2.1 and 2.2, respectively, according to their ranks.

Then, we can compute CPT value as

$$\begin{aligned}
\mathbb{E}_{CPT}(P) &= v_+^\gamma(40 - r_0) \times (w^\beta(1/8) - w^\beta(0)) \\
&+ v_+^\gamma(20 - r_0) \times (w^\beta(3/8) - w^\beta(1/8)) \\
&+ v_-^{\gamma,\lambda}(-50 - r_0) \times (w^\beta(1/8) - w^\beta(0)) \qquad (2.4) \\
&+ v_-^{\gamma,\lambda}(-30 - r_0) \times (w^\beta(11/24) - w^\beta(1/8)) \\
&+ v_-^{\gamma,\lambda}(-10 - r_0) \times (w^\beta(5/8) - w^\beta(11/24)),
\end{aligned}$$

where we can choose v_+^γ, $v_-^{\gamma,\lambda}$, and w^β according to Fig. 2.2. □

2.1.3 Notes

Section 2.1 introduces the EUT and CPT as the benchmark rational and behavioral decision models, respectively. More bounded rationality models can be found in Sect. 4.1.3. Besides decision making under a given environment, an HCPS defender can proactively design mechanisms (e.g., [11, 16, 17, 29]) to induce better decisions from rational or bounded rational decision makers. Moreover, the defender can further design the information available to these decision-makers or the mechanism to generate the information (e.g., the Bayesian persuasion framework [13, 20, 40]) to change their behaviors.

2.2 Game Theory

Decision Theory in Sect. 2.1 studies single-agent decision problems. In contrast, game theory studies multiple agents' decisions within the context of their strategic interactions. The structure of Sect. 2.2 is illustrated in Fig. 2.1.

2.2.1 Basic Game Setting and Elements

A basic static game contains the set of players, defined as $I := \{1, 2, \cdots, I\}$, who interact with each other in one-shot. Each player $i \in I$ has an action set $\mathcal{A}^i$ and a utility function $u^i : \prod_{i \in I} \mathcal{A}^i \mapsto \mathbb{R}$. Similar to (2.1), each utility function u^i maps the consequence of the interaction to real numbers that measures the monetary impact to player $i \in I$. In Example 2.2.1, we illustrate the above basic game setting with the revised version of the defense investment problem in Example 2.1.1.

Example 2.2.1 (Defense Investment Under Strategic Attacks) In contrast to Example 2.1.1, Example 2.2.1 treats attacks as the outcome of an intelligent attacker rather than probabilistic events. Thus, there are two players in Example 2.2.1, i.e., $I = \{D, A\}$, where D represents the SOC defender, and A represents the attacker. The defender has a binary action set $\mathcal{A}^D := \{a_D^D, a_N^D\}$, where a_D^D and a_N^D represent the decision to adopt and not to adopt defense methods, respectively. The attacker also has a binary action set $\mathcal{A}^A := \{a_A^A, a_N^A\}$, where a_A^A and a_N^A represent attacks launched and not launched, respectively. Both players can take two different actions, resulting in four action pairs. The defender and the attacker's utility functions u^D and u^A can thus be represented using two payoff matrices, as shown in Tables 2.3 and 2.4, respectively.

Following Example 2.1.1, we see that the attack and defense incur a cost of c^A and c^D, respectively. An attack succeeds only if defense is not adopted. A successful attack causes damage l^D to the defender and brings benefit l^A to the attacker. Then, we can obtain the utility functions u^D, u^A as follows.

- No attack & No defense: $u^D(a_N^A, a_N^D) = u_{N,N}^D = 0$ and $u^A(a_N^A, a_N^D) = u_{N,N}^A = 0$.

Table 2.3 Defender's payoff matrix u^D

	Attack	No attack
Defense	$u_{D,A}^D$	$u_{D,N}^D$
No defense	$u_{N,A}^D$	$u_{N,N}^D$

Table 2.4 Attack's payoff matrix u^A

	Attack	No attack
Defense	$u_{D,A}^A$	$u_{D,N}^A$
No defense	$u_{N,A}^A$	$u_{N,N}^A$

- No attack & Defense: $u^D(a_N^A, a_D^D) = u_{D,N}^D = -c^D$ and $u^A(a_N^A, a_D^D) = u_{D,N}^A = 0$.
- Attack & No Defense: $u^D(a_A^A, a_N^D) = u_{N,A}^D = -l^D$ and $u^A(a_A^A, a_N^D) = u_{N,A}^A = l^A - c^A$.
- Attack & Defense: $u^D(a_A^A, a_D^D) = u_{D,A}^D = -c^D$ and $u^A(a_A^A, a_D^D) = u_{D,A}^A = -c^A$. □

2.2.2 Mixed Strategy and Nash Equilibrium

The basic game setting in Sect. 2.2.1 assumes that the action sets and utility functions of all players are *common knowledge*.[1] Since a player may predict other players' actions based on their utility functions, each player $i \in I$ adopts a mixed strategy $\sigma^i \in \Delta \mathcal{A}^i$ to make his/her action $a^i \in \mathcal{A}^i$ less predictable.

Let $\sigma^i(a^i) \in [0, 1]$ be the probability of player $i \in I$ taking action $a^i \in \mathcal{A}^i$ and $\sum_{a^i \in \mathcal{A}^i} \sigma^i(a^i) = 1$. Define $\Delta \mathcal{A}$ as the set of probability distributions over $\mathcal{A}$. Define shorthand notations $\sigma^{1:I} \in \Delta \mathcal{A}^{1:I}$ and $a^{1:I} \in \mathcal{A}^{1:I}$ as the tuple of N players' policies $(\sigma^1 \in \Delta \mathcal{A}^1, \sigma^2 \in \Delta \mathcal{A}^2, \cdots, \sigma_N \in \Delta \mathcal{A}^N)$ and actions $(a^1 \in \mathcal{A}^1, a^2 \in \mathcal{A}^2, \cdots, a^N \in \mathcal{A}^N)$, respectively. Then, the expected utility v^i of player $i \in I$ over the I players' mixed strategies $\sigma^{1:I}$ is defined as

$$v^i(\sigma^{1:I}) := \sum_{a^{1:I} \in \mathcal{A}^{1:I}} \prod_{j \in I} \sigma^j(a^j) u^i(a^{1:I}). \tag{2.5}$$

Each player $i \in I$ aims to choose the policy $\sigma^{i,*} \in \Delta \mathcal{A}^i$ that maximizes v^i, which leads to the NE defined in Definition 2.3. Let the shorthand notations a^{-i} and σ^{-i} denote the actions and strategies of players other than P_i, respectively.

Definition 2.3 (Nash Equilibrium (NE)) The set of N players' policies $\sigma^{1:I,*} \in \Delta \mathcal{A}^{1:I}$ comprises a mixed-strategy NE if

$$v^i(\sigma^{i,*}, \sigma^{-i,*}) \geq v^i(\sigma^i, \sigma^{-i,*}), \forall \sigma^i \in \Delta \mathcal{A}^i, \forall i \in I. \tag{2.6}$$

Based on the definition, there is no advantage to deviate from an NE if other players follow it. Thus, NE provides a reliable prediction of the interaction outcome. Mixed-strategy NE of the basic game in Sect. 2.2.1 can be computed by linear programming [3].

---

[1] There is *common knowledge* of p in a group of agents G when all the agents in G know p they all know that they know p, they all know that they all know that they know p, and so on ad infinitum.

2.2.3 Notes

Section 2.2 introduces the essential concept of Nash Equilibrium (NE) in one-shot non-cooperative games with finite action sets and complete information. We can extend NE to correlated equilibrium, non-cooperative games to cooperative games, one-shot games to dynamic games, finite games to infinite games, complete information to incomplete information, etc. Readers are encouraged to classical books (e.g., [3, 10, 28]) for more information on these game models and the algorithmic aspects to compute the equilibrium. Moreover, we can extend the above to formulate games with more complex structures such as finite-horizon semi-Markov games [43], mean-field games [21, 35], games-in-games [8, 44], network games [25, 45], signaling games [7, 30], dynamic Bayesian games [18, 34] in connection with HCPS security and resilience. Game theory has been widely applied to HCPS in diverse scenarios including power and energy systems [9, 24], critical infrastructures [31, 32], autonomous vehicles [36, 42], cyber insurance [39, 41], and communication networks [46, 47]. Rationality is the key assumption in many game-theoretic frameworks. Several extensions of game theory that incorporate human behaviors will be discussed in later chapters, including bounded rationality in Sect. 4.1.3.4, Theory of Mind (ToM) in Sect. 3.3.2, and incentives in Sect. 4.2.2.

2.3 Learning Theory

System-scientific models of HCPS face the challenges of incomplete information that arise from adversarial deception, external noise, and the inadequate knowledge of the other players' behaviors and goals. Bayesian learning in Sect. 2.3.1 and Reinforcement Learning (RL) in Sect. 2.3.2 are two quintessential learning schemes to acquire intelligence (e.g., better state estimation and improved control strategies). The structure of Sect. 2.3 is illustrated in Fig. 2.1.

2.3.1 Bayesian Learning

Consider a random variable X with support $\mathcal{X}$. We can treat the prospect P in Sect. 2.1 as the prior belief of X. Let Y be another random variable with support $\mathcal{Y} := \{y_1, y_2, \cdots, y_m\}, m \in \mathbb{N}$. Suppose that we have a prior knowledge of the conditional probability $\Pr(Y|X)$. An observation of Y's realization brings additional information about X's realization, which leads to the posterior belief of X via the Bayesian rule in (2.7).

$$\Pr(x_i|y_j) = \frac{\Pr(y_j|x_i)p_i}{\Pr(y_j)}, \Pr(y_j) \neq 0, \forall i \in \{1, \cdots, n\}, j \in \{1, \cdots, m\}. \quad (2.7)$$

We can compute $\Pr(y_j)$ via the *law of total probability*, i.e.,

$$\Pr(y_j) = \sum_{i=1}^{n} \Pr(y_j|x_i)p_i, \ \forall j \in \{1, \cdots, m\}. \tag{2.8}$$

Following Example 2.1.1, we construct Example 2.3.1 to illustrate the procedure of Bayesian learning.

Example 2.3.1 Consider an Intrusion Detection System (IDS) with a binary outcome $Y = \{y_D, y_N\}$, where y_D and y_N denote whether attacks are detected or not, respectively. Since the IDS is imperfect, false alarms and misdetection happen with probability $p_F \in [0, 1]$ and $p_M \in [0, 1]$, respectively. Figure 2.3 depicts the conditional probability $Pr(Y|X)$.

Suppose that defense is adopted, and the prior distribution of X is P. Following (2.7) and (2.8), given a positive detection result y_D, the attack is successful with probability $\Pr(x_S|y_D) = \frac{(1-p_M)p_A}{(1-p_M)p_A+p_F(1-p_A)}$; given a negative detection result y_N, the attack succeeds with probability $\Pr(x_S|y_N) = \frac{p_M p_A}{p_M p_A+(1-p_F)(1-p_A)}$. □

2.3.2 Reinforcement Learning

In Sect. 2.1, the uncertainty is one-shot and fully described by the prospect P. However, since HCPSs are dynamic systems, the uncertainty in the environment changes persistently. System-scientific models usually incorporate the dynamic uncertainty into a system state $X \in \mathcal{X}$ that changes probabilistically over discrete stages indexed by $k \in \mathbb{Z}^+$. While interacting with the environment, the RL agent observes the sequential realization of states $\{\bar{x}^k\}_{k\in\mathbb{Z}^+}$, obtains rewards $\{\bar{u}^k\}_{k\in\mathbb{Z}^+}$,

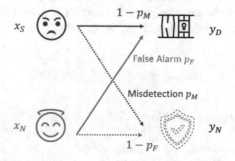

Fig. 2.3 The imperfect IDS with false alarm rate p_F and misdetection rate p_M, respectively. The red and blue faces on the left represent the binary state X of whether the attack is successful or not. The solid and dashed icons on the right represent the binary state Y of whether the detection result is positive or negative

and learns to take the optimal sequence of actions $\{\bar{a}^k\}_{k\in\mathbb{Z}^+}$ from a finite action set $\mathcal{A}$.

Having been actively studied for decades, RL has an extensive library of algorithms that help the agent find a satisfactory policy. They can be classified as model-based and model-free RL based on whether the agent attempts to predict the environmental parameters. The model-free RL also has two main categories for optimizing the policy: value-based and policy-based methods. We provide a sketch of the Q-learning algorithm as a typical value-based, model-free RL scheme.

Q-learning makes use of the "Q" function, which is a value-action function Q : $\mathcal{X} \times \mathcal{A} \to \mathbb{R}^+$. Assuming that the reward $\bar{u}^k \in \mathbb{R}$ at each stage $k \in \mathbb{Z}^+$ is determined through a reward function $\tilde{u} : \mathcal{X} \times \mathcal{A} \mapsto \mathbb{R}$, the Q-learning algorithm seeks the optimal Q-values $Q^*(\bar{x}, \bar{a})$ that satisfy the Bellman equation [5] under a discounted factor $\gamma_d \in (0, 1]$, i.e.,

$$Q(\bar{x}, \bar{a}) = \tilde{u}(\bar{x}, \bar{a}) + \gamma_d \sum_{s'} f_{tr}(\bar{x}, \bar{x}', \bar{a}) \min_{\bar{a}' \in \mathcal{A}} Q(\bar{x}', \bar{a}'), \quad \text{for } \bar{x} \in \mathcal{X}, \bar{a} \in \mathcal{A},$$

(2.9)

where $f_{tr}(\bar{x}, \bar{x}', \bar{a})$ is the probability that the HCPS state at the next stage is $\bar{x}'$, given the current state $\bar{x}$ and the current action $\bar{a}$. Without the knowledge of the transition probability f_{tr} and the reward function $\tilde{u}$, the RL agent can instead learn its estimated Q-values $Q^k(\bar{x}^k, \bar{a}^k), \forall \bar{x}^k \in \mathcal{X}, \bar{a}^k \in \mathcal{A}$, at each stage $k \in \mathbb{Z}^+$, by interacting with the environment, i.e.,

$$Q^{k+1}(\bar{x}^k, \bar{a}^k) = Q^k(\bar{x}^k, \bar{a}^k) + \alpha^k(\bar{x}^k, \bar{a}^k)$$
$$\cdot \left[\gamma_d \min_{\bar{a}'} Q^k(\bar{x}^{k+1}, \bar{a}') + \bar{u}^k - Q^k(\bar{x}^k, \bar{a}^k) \right],$$

(2.10)

where the sequences of states $\{\bar{x}^k\}_{k\in\mathbb{Z}^+}$, and rewards $\{\bar{u}^k\}_{k\in\mathbb{Z}^+}$ are obtained from the environment, while the sequence of actions $\{\bar{a}^k\}_{k\in\mathbb{Z}^+}$ are chosen by the agent. By properly choosing the learning rate α^k according to Condition 1, the Q-learning algorithm converges *in probability*. Then, we can obtain the optimal action $\bar{a}^*(\bar{x})$ at each state $\bar{x} \in \mathcal{X}$ as

$$\bar{a}^*(\bar{x}) \in \min_{\bar{a}' \in \mathcal{A}} Q^*(\bar{x}, \bar{a}'), \forall \bar{x} \in \mathcal{X}.$$

(2.11)

Condition 1 (Convergence Condition) When the learning rate $\alpha^k(\bar{x}^k, \bar{a}^k) \in (0, 1)$ satisfies $\sum_{k=0}^{\infty} \alpha^k(\bar{x}^k, \bar{a}^k) = \infty$, $\sum_{k=0}^{\infty} (\alpha^k(\bar{x}^k, \bar{a}^k))^2 < \infty$, $\forall \bar{x}^k \in \mathcal{X}, \forall \bar{a}^k \in \mathcal{A}$, and all state-action pairs are explored infinitely, $Q^k(\bar{x}^k, \bar{a}^k)$ converges to the optimal Q-value $Q^*(\bar{x}^k, \bar{a}^k)$ for all $\bar{x}^k \in \mathcal{X}, \bar{a}^k \in \mathcal{A}$ with probability 1 as $k \to \infty$.   □

After the Q-value is updated at each stage $k \in \mathbb{Z}^+$, the RL agent can choose an action $\bar{a}^k$ to implement at stage $k + 1$ based on a feasible exploration policy that guarantees the infinite exploration of all state-action pairs to satisfy the convergence condition. Among all the feasible exploration policies, we seek the one with *sufficient exploration efficiency*. As the RL agent explores the environment to accumulate information, he can also exploit the acquired information to choose actions that provide more reward in future stages. In Condition 2, we introduce the ϵ-greedy policy as a feasible exploration policy that keeps a tradeoff between exploration and exploitation.

Condition 2 (ϵ-Greedy Exploration Policy) At each stage $k \in \mathbb{Z}^+$, the ϵ-greedy exploration policy means that the RL agent selects a random action in $\mathcal{A}$ with probability $\epsilon^k \in [0, 1]$, and the optimal current-stage action $\arg\min_{\bar{a}' \in \mathcal{A}} Q^k(\bar{x}^k, \bar{a}')$ with probability $1 - \epsilon^k$. □

We can choose ϵ^k as a constant $\epsilon \in (0, 1]$ over stages $k \in \mathbb{Z}^+$. We can also gradually decrease the value of ϵ^k to encourage more exploitation as k increases.

2.3.3 Notes

Learning theory is a broad area of research that includes supervised, unsupervised, and semi-supervised learning. In supervised and semi-supervised learning, high-quality data with labels require human annotators. The human attention vulnerability may lead to labeling errors, which will be discussed later in Sect. 4.1.1.1. The RL algorithms in Sect. 2.3.2 can integrate with game theory and lead to multi-agent RL [6, 22, 23]. Its connection with deep learning gives rise to deep RL [1].

In an adversarial environment, attackers can compromise learning algorithms, the training data, and the data labels. Thus, adversarial machine learning [12, 14, 15, 38] has been introduced to study such attacks and the defenses against them.

To reduce the training cost, transfer learning and meta-learning [48] are proposed to transfer knowledge gained in one task to a different but related problem. Other areas of investigation in learning include ethics issues and fairness [26], explainability [33], federated machine learning [37], and quantum learning [2].

References

1. Arulkumaran K, Deisenroth MP, Brundage M, Bharath AA (2017) Deep reinforcement learning: a brief survey. IEEE Signal Process Mag 34(6):26–38
2. Arunachalam S, de Wolf R (2017) Guest column: a survey of quantum learning theory. ACM Sigact News 48(2):41–67
3. Başar T, Olsder GJ (1998) Dynamic noncooperative game theory. SIAM, Philadelphia
4. Bernoulli D (1954) Exposition of a new theory on the measurement of risk. Econometrica 22(1):23–36. http://www.jstor.org/stable/1909829
5. Bertsekas D, Tsitsiklis JN (1996) Neuro-dynamic programming. Athena Scientific, Nashua
6. Busoniu L, Babuska R, De Schutter B (2008) A comprehensive survey of multiagent reinforcement learning. IEEE Trans Syst Man Cybern C Appl Rev 38(2):156–172

7. Casey W, Morales JA, Wright E, Zhu Q, Mishra B (2016) Compliance signaling games: toward modeling the deterrence of insider threats. Comput Math Organ Theory 22(3):318–349

8. Chen J, Zhu Q (2019) Control of multilayer mobile autonomous systems in adversarial environments: a games-in-games approach. IEEE Trans Control Netw Syst 7(3):1056–1068

9. Chen J, Zhu Q (2022) A cross-layer design approach to strategic cyber defense and robust switching control of cyber-physical wind energy systems. IEEE Trans Autom Sci Eng 20:624–635

10. Fudenberg D, Tirole J (1991) Game theory. MIT Press, Cambridge

11. Horák K, Zhu Q, Bošanský B (2017) Manipulating adversary's belief: a dynamic game approach to deception by design for proactive network security. In: International conference on decision and game theory for security. Springer, Berlin, pp 273–294

12. Huang Y, Zhu Q (2019) Deceptive reinforcement learning under adversarial manipulations on cost signals. In: International conference on decision and game theory for security. Springer, Berlin, pp 217–237

13. Huang L, Zhu Q (2021) Duplicity games for deception design with an application to insider threat mitigation. IEEE Trans Inf Forensics Secur 16:4843–4856

14. Huang Y, Zhu Q (2021) Manipulating reinforcement learning: stealthy attacks on cost signals. In: Game theory and machine learning for cyber security. Wiley, Hoboken, pp 367–388

15. Huang L, Joseph AD, Nelson B, Rubinstein BI, Tygar JD (2011) Adversarial machine learning. In: Proceedings of the 4th ACM workshop on security and artificial intelligence, pp 43–58

16. Huang L, Chen J, Zhu Q (2017) A factored MDP approach to optimal mechanism design for resilient large-scale interdependent critical infrastructures. In: 2017 workshop on Modeling and Simulation of Cyber-Physical Energy Systems (MSCPES). IEEE, pp 1–6

17. Huang L, Chen J, Zhu Q (2018) Factored Markov game theory for secure interdependent infrastructure networks. In: Game theory for security and risk management. Birkhäuser, Cham, pp 99–126

18. Huang Y, Chen J, Huang L, Zhu Q (2020) Dynamic games for secure and resilient control system design. Natl Sci Rev 7(7):1125–1141

19. Kahneman D, Tversky A (1979) Prospect theory: an analysis of decision under risk. Econometrica: J Econ Soc 47:263–291

20. Kamenica E, Gentzkow M (2011) Bayesian persuasion. Am Econ Rev 101(6):2590–2615

21. Kolokoltsov VN, Bensoussan A (2016) Mean-field-game model for Botnet defense in cybersecurity. Appl Math Optim 74(3):669–692

22. Li T, Peng G, Zhu Q, Başar T (2022) The confluence of networks, games, and learning a game-theoretic framework for multiagent decision making over networks. IEEE Control Syst Mag 42(4):35–67

23. Li T, Zhao Y, Zhu Q (2022) The role of information structures in game-theoretic multi-agent learning. Annu Rev Control 53:296–314

24. Maharjan S, Zhu Q, Zhang Y, Gjessing S, Basar T (2013) Dependable demand response management in the smart grid: a Stackelberg game approach. IEEE Trans Smart Grid 4(1):120–132

25. Manshaei MH, Zhu Q, Alpcan T, Bacşar T, Hubaux JP (2013) Game theory meets network security and privacy. ACM Comput Surv 45(3):1–39

26. Mehrabi N, Morstatter F, Saxena N, Lerman K, Galstyan A (2021) A survey on bias and fairness in machine learning. ACM Comput Surv 54(6):1–35

27. Morgenstern O, Von Neumann J (1953) Theory of games and economic behavior. Princeton University Press, Princeton

28. Owen G (2013) Game theory. Emerald Group Publishing, Bingley

29. Pawlick J, Zhu Q (2017) Proactive defense against physical denial of service attacks using Poisson signaling games. In: International conference on decision and game theory for security. Springer, Berlin, pp 336–356

30. Pawlick J, Colbert E, Zhu Q (2018) Modeling and analysis of leaky deception using signaling games with evidence. IEEE Trans Inf Forensics Secur 14(7):1871–1886

31. Rass S, Schauer S (2018) Game theory for security and risk management. Springer International Publishing. https://doi.org/10.1007/978-3-319-75268-6
32. Rass S, Schauer S, König S, Zhu Q (2020) Cyber-security in critical infrastructures. Springer, Berlin
33. Roscher R, Bohn B, Duarte MF, Garcke J (2020) Explainable machine learning for scientific insights and discoveries. IEEE Access 8:42200–42216
34. Smidts C, Ray I, Zhu Q, Vaddi PK, Zhao Y, Huang L, Diao X, Talukdar R, Pietrykowski MC (2022) Cyber-security threats and response models in nuclear power plants. Springer, Cham
35. Wang Y, Yu FR, Tang H, Huang M (2014) A mean field game theoretic approach for security enhancements in mobile ad hoc networks. IEEE Trans Wirel Commun 13(3):1616–1627
36. Xu Z, Zhu Q (2015) A cyber-physical game framework for secure and resilient multi-agent autonomous systems. In: 2015 54th IEEE Conference on Decision and Control (CDC). IEEE, pp 5156–5161
37. Yang Q, Liu Y, Chen T, Tong Y (2019) Federated machine learning: concept and applications. ACM Trans Intell Syst Technol 10(2):1–19
38. Zhang R, Zhu Q (2015) Secure and resilient distributed machine learning under adversarial environments. In: 2015 18th International conference on information fusion (Fusion). IEEE, pp 644–651
39. Zhang R, Zhu Q (2021) Optimal cyber-insurance contract design for dynamic risk management and mitigation. IEEE Trans Comput Soc Syst 9:1087–1100
40. Zhang T, Zhu Q (2021) On the equilibrium elicitation of Markov games through information design. arXiv preprint arXiv:210207152
41. Zhang R, Zhu Q, Hayel Y (2017) A bi-level game approach to attack-aware cyber insurance of computer networks. IEEE J Sel Areas Commun 35(3):779–794
42. Zhao Y, Zhu Q (2022) Stackelberg meta-learning for strategic guidance in multi-robot trajectory planning. arXiv preprint arXiv:221113336
43. Zhao Y, Huang L, Smidts C, Zhu Q (2020) Finite-horizon semi-Markov game for time-sensitive attack response and probabilistic risk assessment in nuclear power plants. Reliab Eng Syst Saf 201:106878
44. Zhu Q, Basar T (2015) Game-theoretic methods for robustness, security, and resilience of cyberphysical control systems: games-in-games principle for optimal cross-layer resilient control systems. IEEE Control Syst Mag 35(1):46–65
45. Zhu Q, Tembine H, Başar T (2010) Network security configurations: a nonzero-sum stochastic game approach. In: Proceedings of the 2010 American control conference. IEEE, pp 1059–1064
46. Zhu Q, Saad W, Han Z, Poor HV, Başar T (2011) Eavesdropping and jamming in next-generation wireless networks: a game-theoretic approach. In: 2011-MILCOM 2011 military communications conference. IEEE, pp 119–124
47. Zhu Q, Clark A, Poovendran R, Başar T (2012) Deceptive routing games. In: 2012 IEEE 51st IEEE Conference on Decision and Control (CDC). IEEE, pp 2704–2711
48. Zhuang F, Qi Z, Duan K, Xi D, Zhu Y, Zhu H, Xiong H, He Q (2020) A comprehensive survey on transfer learning. Proc IEEE 109(1):43–76

Chapter 3
Cognitive Capacities for Designing, Operating, Supervising, and Securing Complex Systems

Abstract Despite the integration of a variety of "Industry 4.0" technologies, the active presence of human actors is required to bring their cognitive capabilities to *Designing*, *Operating*, *Supervising*, and *Securing* (DOSS) complex systems. Figure 3.1 illustrates the structure of Chap. 3. In particular, we discuss *situation awareness* in Sect. 3.1, *problem solving* in Sect. 3.2, and *collaboration* in Sect. 3.3 as the three essential cognitive capabilities that distinguish a human actor from a traditional cyber-physical component in the above DOSS procedures. Examples of human roles in four DOSS procedures are introduced to illustrate these three classes of cognitive capabilities and are mapped onto the four quadrants in Fig. 3.2 based on their time-sensitivity and interactivity.

Keywords Situation awareness · Problem solving · Decision making · Domain knowledge · Theory of mind · Order of intentionality · Belief hierarchy

3.1 Situation Awareness

As shown in Fig. 3.1, Situation Awareness (SA) is the first pillar to support the human roles of designing, supervising, operating, and securing complex systems. SA is the perception of the elements in the environment within a volume of time and space, the comprehension of their meaning, and the projection of their status in the near future (Fig. 3.1). SA is a distinguishable cognitive ability consisting of knowledge acquisition, refinement, and utilization, and it can be affected by a variety of human factors, including attention and working memory. SA enables humans to accomplish time-critical tasks, including field operation and system configuration, alert inspection, and technical support, as shown in Fig. 3.2. Following the definition in [5], Sect. 3.1 presents the three levels of SA.

Fig. 3.1 The structure of
Chap. 3 concerning three
classes of cognitive
capabilities as the pillars to
support four classes of human
roles

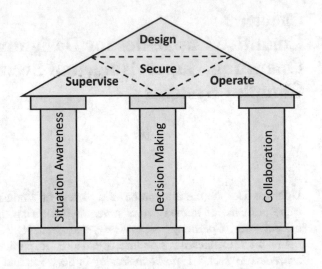

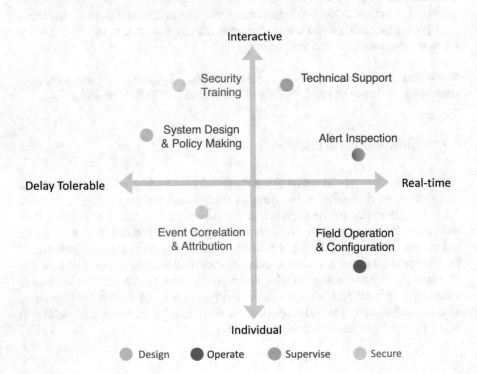

Fig. 3.2 The four-quadrant classification of human roles in designing, operating, supervising, and securing complex systems are depicted in green, blue, orange, and yellow, respectively. The *x*-axis and *y*-axis represent the time-sensitiveness and the interactivity of these roles, respectively

3.1.1 Perception of the Elements in the Environment

The first level of SA is to perceive the status, attributes, and dynamics of relevant elements in the environment, which are closely associated with the cognitive processes of sensation and attention in Fig. 1.4. For example, in the control room of a nuclear power plant, an operator would attend to the readings from various sensors to know the status of the power plant (e.g., temperature, pressure, and production rate). Meanwhile, they receive messages and alerts acoustically and visually, which require timely responses to prevent failures and attacks. During the perception process, human operators perform a triage process by assigning different levels of attention to all those stimuli. The perception SA demonstrates the human's cognitive ability for monitoring, recognition, and categorization.

3.1.2 Comprehension of the Current Situation

Associated with memory and mental operations in Fig. 1.4, the second level of SA is to form a holistic understanding of the current situation by synthesizing the perceived elements. The understanding depends on domain knowledge, reasoning, and common sense. For example, the operator in the control room needs to determine the current status of the plant based on the readings, log files, and alerts. The operator's decisions include whether the alerts are associated with disturbances, faults, or attacks, what the impacts and risks of these events are, and how time-sensitive the events are. They lead to the acquisition and refinement of knowledge. Although the wide application of high-accuracy sensors in CPS may fulfill the perception level of SA, questions at those high abstraction levels can only be answered by experienced operators.

3.1.3 Projection of Future Status

Established on the first two levels of SA, the third level consists of the ability to project the future status of the elements in the environment and form responsive strategies. The ability depends on the utilization of existing domain knowledge, its application to the current scenario, and the prediction of the complex and dynamic CPS process. For example, after the operator recognizes that the power plant is under attacks, he needs to use defensive responses to protect the system from large-scale failures and deter follow-up attacks. The selection and evaluation of the response strategies depend on the current situation and goals, which demonstrate the cognitive capabilities of goal-directed planning (i.e., carrying out steps to achieve the ultimate goal), prediction, and knowledge abstraction and creation.

3.2 Problem Solving and Decision Making

SA in Sect. 3.1 lays a critical foundation for dynamic decision-making and problem-solving whose outcome directly affects the cyber-physical processes, as shown in Fig. 1.2. Serving as the second pillar in Fig. 3.1 to support the four human roles, problem-solving and decision-making are required in almost all tasks in Fig. 3.2, including event correlation for cyber attribution, policy design, and system configuration. The advancement of AI and big data has improved machines' ability to solve specific problems. However, they are far from having the human capabilities to solve general problems creatively and adaptively. Human capabilities of flexibility and creativity, as described in Sect. 3.2.1, refer to humans' ability to devise alternative plans in *a given environment*. In contrast, adaptability and learning in Sect. 3.2.2 refer to the ability of humans to adapt and respond to *changing circumstances*.

3.2.1 Flexibility and Creativity

Every coin has two sides. Humans are less dependable than computers at following instructions, which brings flexibility and creativity to solving problems and making decisions. The flexibility results from level-2 SA. Based on their understanding of the ultimate goal and the impacts of different actions, humans can carry out alternative plans to achieve the goal. While carrying out these alternative plans, humans can go through the following three processes to develop insights, as shown in Sternberg et al. [12].

- Selective encoding to filter irrelevant information.
- Selective comparison to draw connections between the acquired knowledge and the new experiences.
- Selective combination to understand different components and put them together effectively and systematically.

These insights lead to innovative solutions that are *new* (e.g., containing novel Tactics, Techniques, and Procedures (TTP)) and *appropriate* (e.g., satisfying the constraints of the current problem). In HCPSs, the flexibility and creativity of problem-solving and decision-making enable them for network management, configuration, and design, including routing design [10] and firewall configurations [14].

3.2.2 Adaptability and Learning

Intelligent agents in dynamic environments need to frequently modify existing plans and strategies in response to unanticipated changes. An operator in the control room needs to adapt to numerous scenarios that cannot be completely covered by pre-training or exactly-matched procedures. A driver needs to identify signs correctly regardless of various weather conditions, partial obstruction, and distortion. We have seen the failures of autonomous driving algorithms in recognizing a stop sign that is slightly distorted or covered by some stickers [6], while humans have no problems in recognizing the distorted stop sign.

Domain knowledge is one of the essential factors that make humans experts at adapting to unforeseen circumstances, even if they have not been specifically trained under these circumstances. The authors in [3] use video games as an example to demonstrate the role of human prior knowledge (e.g., a key needs to be collected before opening a door, a ladder can be climbed to reach different platforms, collecting coins provides benefits, etc.). The results show that masking semantics, object identities, affordances, and similarities significantly hurts human performance (measured by the average number of deaths and average time to win).

Each adaptation to unknown circumstances provides feedback, which further helps humans expand their domain knowledge. The learning process transforms a novice into an expert and further improves his/her adaptability in the future. In contrast to the current machine learning algorithms that are usually set to learn a specific task, humans have the general ability to learn heterogeneous tasks.

3.3 Collaboration

As shown in Fig. 3.1, collaboration is the third pillar to support the four roles. Ranging from the operation of nuclear power plants to the analysis of alerts, many modern CPS scenarios are of high cognitive complexity and demand effective teamwork. As social animals, humans excel at collaboration. The collaboration makes one plus one greater than two and achieves social intelligence. Human collaborations rely on two essential cognitive abilities, i.e., interacting with others to deliver information and understanding others' mental status, as shown in Sects. 3.3.1 and 3.3.2, respectively. In Fig. 3.2, human roles with higher levels of interactivity, including security training and technical support, depend more on these collabora-tion capabilities.

3.3.1 Interaction and Communication

The ones who have interacted with *Alexa* or *Siri* may have experienced confronta-tions resulting from the misunderstanding of AI, even though every word has been correctly identified. The misunderstanding can lead to damages in HCPSs. For example, when a human operator speaks to a robot:

Could you turn off the machine within 10 seconds?

Then, a robot may not understand the operator's hidden intention to actually turn off the machine but simply answer "Yes, I can" without taking any action. On the contrary, humans can easily understand verbal and body language. Besides understanding the content, we can also perceive the emotions, hidden intentions, and even personalities based on the interaction and communication with others. These skills enable humans to fulfill highly interactive tasks. For example, during security training, the trainer needs to evaluate the effectiveness of the course based on the trainees' responses, e.g., whether they look confused. Then, the trainer can change the content and the delivery methods adaptively, e.g., by repeating or giving examples.

3.3.2 Theory of Mind

Theory of Mind (ToM) refers to the capacity to understand other people by ascribing mental states to them. When humans work as a team to solve a task, ToM enables them to develop approximate models of the goals and capabilities of each other, facilitate the formation of trust, and support fluid team performance. For example, to provide technical support, the customer representative needs to think from the customer's perspective to figure out the issue and potential solutions.

ToM is an advanced cognitive capability acquired in childhood. As shown in the celebrated *Sally-Anne's task*, until around four years old, children usually cannot develop the ability to take others' perspectives and predict others' beliefs that are inconsistent with reality. We present the following example to illustrate ToM, as shown in Fig. 3.3. When operator Anna asks operator Bob to turn off the machine after the current task C is finished, Bob may not follow the instruction because another operator, Eva, told him several minutes ago that the machine is assigned another task D when task C is finished. Bob makes the decision not to follow because he knows the additional information, and he further knows that Anna does not know the additional information. Therefore, Bob understands that Anna has formed a false belief due to a lack of information, and he should not follow her instruction made under the false belief.

In this example illustrated in Fig. 3.3, Anna's direct demand to turn off the machine is referred to as the *first-order intentionality* in ToM. Bob's understanding of Anna's mental state (i.e., "Bob thinks that Anna thinks that task C is the last task") is referred to as the *second-order intentionality*. Besides, Eva knows that she has told Bob but not Anna of task D, and Eva further knows that Bob understands the asymmetric information between him and Anna. Therefore, Eva should be able to infer Bob's mental state about Anna's mental state (i.e., "Eva thinks that Bob thinks that Anna thinks that task C is the last task") and predict that Bob will not follow Anna's instruction, which is referred to as *third-order intentionality*. Analogously, *higher-order intentionality* can be defined through the recursive understanding of mental states, or equivalently, a hierarchy of beliefs. Note that besides among three or more agents in the machine turn-off example, higher-order intentionality can be

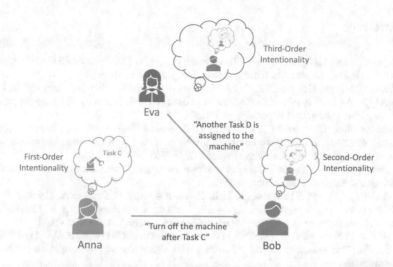

Fig. 3.3 The illustration of the ToM example and the order of intentionality. Anna has the *first-order intentionality* that the machine should be turned off because Task C is going to finish. Bob has the *second-order intentionality* that Anna has a false belief due to a lack of information, so the machine should not be turned off. Eva has the *third-order intentionality* that Bob should know about Anna's false belief and thus not turn off the machine

defined between as few as two agents; e.g., "I think that you suppose that I intend that you believe that something will happen."

Many system-scientific models have been established to understand ToM, including the Bayesian theory of mind [1] and game theory of mind [15]. The asymmetric knowledge (e.g., Bob but not Anna knows the additional task D), the distinction between mutual knowledge and common knowledge, and the belief hierarchy in ToM lead to rich game theory models and concepts, including hypergames [2], epistemological game theory [8], and level-k reasoning in Sect. 4.1.3.4. Besides establishing models to understand ToM, researchers have further used meta-learning to build a Theory of Mind neural network (ToMnet) that passes the "Sally-Anne" test of recognizing that others can hold false beliefs about the world [9].

3.4 Discussions

A comprehensive list of individual, interpersonal, and social cognitive capabilities to enhance HCPSs is beyond the scope of Chap. 3. For more details about other cognitive capabilities and the theory behind them, we refer readers to books on cognitive science (e.g., Thagard [13]) and cognitive psychology (e.g., Solso et al. [11]). For detailed modeling and analysis of human behaviors, factors, and capabilities in sociotechnical systems and human-in-the-loop systems, we refer readers to review papers on human-centric manufacturing, such as [4, 7].

References

1. Baker CL, Jara-Ettinger J, Saxe R, Tenenbaum JB (2017) Rational quantitative attribution of beliefs, desires and percepts in human mentalizing. Nat Hum Behav 1(4):1–10
2. Bennett PG (1980) Hypergames: developing a model of conflict. Futures 12(6):489–507
3. Dubey R, Agrawal P, Pathak D, Griffiths TL, Efros AA (2018) Investigating human priors for playing video games. arXiv preprint arXiv:180210217
4. Emmanouilidis C, Pistofidis P, Bertoncelj L, Katsouros V, Fournaris A, Koulamas C, Ruiz-Carcel C (2019) Enabling the human in the loop: linked data and knowledge in industrial cyber-physical systems. Annu Rev Control 47:249–265
5. Endsley MR (2017) Toward a theory of situation awareness in dynamic systems. In: Situational awareness. Routledge, Abingdon, pp 9–42
6. Eykholt K, Evtimov I, Fernandes E, Li B, Rahmati A, Xiao C, Prakash A, Kohno T, Song D (2018) Robust physical-world attacks on deep learning visual classification. In: Proceedings of the IEEE conference on computer vision and pattern recognition, pp 1625–1634
7. Fantini P, Pinzone M, Taisch M (2020) Placing the operator at the centre of industry 4.0 design: modelling and assessing human activities within cyber-physical systems. Comput Ind Eng 139:105058
8. Perea A (2012) Epistemic game theory: reasoning and choice. Cambridge University Press, Cambridge
9. Rabinowitz N, Perbet F, Song F, Zhang C, Eslami SA, Botvinick M (2018) Machine theory of mind. In: International conference on machine learning, PMLR, pp 4218–4227
10. Roscoe T, Hand S, Isaacs R, Mortier R, Jardetzky P (2003) Predicate routing: enabling controlled networking. ACM SIGCOMM Comput Commun Rev 33(1):65–70
11. Solso RL, MacLin MK, MacLin OH (2005) Cognitive psychology. Pearson Education New Zealand, North Shore City
12. Sternberg RJ, Davidson JE, et al (2005) Conceptions of giftedness, vol 2. Cambridge University Press, New York, NY
13. Thagard P (2005) Mind: introduction to cognitive science. MIT Press, Cambridge
14. Wool A (2004) The use and usability of direction-based filtering in firewalls. Comput Secur 23(6):459–468
15. Yoshida W, Dolan RJ, Friston KJ (2008) Game theory of mind. PLoS Comput Biol 4(12):e1000254

Chapter 4
Review of System-Scientific Perspectives for Analysis, Exploitation, and Mitigation of Cognitive Vulnerabilities

Abstract Chapter 3 elaborates on three critical types of human cognitive capabilities to fulfill four classes of CPS tasks in Fig. 3.2. For all of its advantages, the active presence of human cognition also brings vulnerabilities. Compared to computer programs and robots that strictly follow the algorithms and retain the same level of performance, human operators may violate security procedures or be prone to errors due to misaligned incentives, herding effects, inattention, fatigue, and bounded rationality.

In Chap. 4, we classify cognitive vulnerabilities into innate vulnerabilities in Sect. 4.1 and acquired vulnerabilities in Sect. 4.2 based on whether they can be mitigated through short-term external interference, including security training and mechanism design in Fig. 1.8. For each cognitive vulnerability, we first illustrate its impact on HCPSs and how cognitive attacks can exploit it. Then, we present system-scientific perspectives to characterize the vulnerability, the attacks, and the defense methods in different security scenarios, which focus on the computational aspects of vulnerability analysis, exploitation, and mitigation in the literature.

Keywords Innate vulnerability · Acquired vulnerability · Bounded rationality · Misaligned incentive · Security awareness · Incompliance · Inattentional blindness · Active learning · Rational inattention

4.1 Innate Vulnerabilities

In Sect. 4.1, we introduce vulnerabilities of attention, risk perception, and decision-making as three classes of innate vulnerabilities in Sects. 4.1.1, 4.1.2, and 4.1.3, respectively. Since we usually cannot mitigate innate vulnerabilities by changing humans directly (e.g., through short-term training and security education), most of the cognitive reliability and cognitive security methods focus on designing AI enhancers shown in Fig. 1.8.

4.1.1 Attention Vulnerability

We illustrate different perspectives on attention vulnerabilities through the following three common scenarios in HCPSs. Phishing in Sect. 4.1.1.2 and alert fatigue in Sect. 4.1.1.3 result from inattention and cognitive overload, respectively, while errors in hand-labeled data in Sect. 4.1.1.1 can result from both.

4.1.1.1 Human Annotators and Labeling Errors

We have demonstrated the close integration of AI into HCPSs in Sect. 1.1.2. The success of AI algorithms (particularly supervised and semi-supervised learning algorithms) heavily relies on a sizable amount of data with high-quality labels. However, the label quality depends on the human annotators, which brings in much uncertainty due to various cognitive vulnerabilities, including inattention.

The authors in [51] find that an average of at least 3.3% labeling errors can be found across the ten of the most-cited (i.e., cited more than 100,000 times) datasets.[1] Among a range of human vulnerabilities, including *search satisfying*, *overconfidence*, and *confirmation bias* [43], cognitive overload and inattention of the human annotators can significantly contribute to these labeling errors. For example, the annotator may fail to place a label around one or more pedestrians if the annotator isn't observant enough or there are overwhelming tag lists [75]. Cognitive reliability methods mitigate this type of attentional vulnerability through the following four perspectives.

- Human computation [59] gathers the potentially wasted human cognition resources to generate labels; e.g., reCAPTCHA [80] generates labels for scanned words that an Optical Character Reader (OCR) fails to recognize when humans use CAPTCHA (Completely Automated Public Turing test to tell Computers and Human Apart) to "prove" they are human.
- Human-augmenting labeling systems (e.g., [78]) reduce the workload of human annotators by learning from humans and automatically generating labels. As shown in Fig. 4.1, after human annotators label some data, AI can learn from these hand-labeled data to label the remaining unlabeled data in red.
- Active learning [70] and active semi-supervised learning (e.g., [93]) allows the algorithm to actively select the data to learn. Since active learning can achieve greater accuracy with fewer labeled training instances, it reduces the total labeling workload, as shown in Fig. 4.2. In the third box of hand-labeled data, active learning discards the unlabeled data, while active semi-supervised learning further exploits the structure of the remaining unlabeled data.
- *Confident learning* [50, 51] evaluates label quality by characterizing and identifying label errors in datasets, enabling a label correction.

---

[1] Test set errors across the 10 datasets can be viewed at https://labelerrors.com.

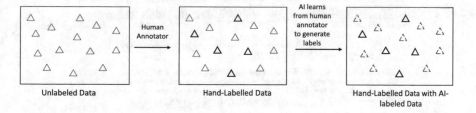

Fig. 4.1 Human-augmented labeling systems learn from human annotators to generate labels automatically. The dotted and solid black triangles represent the unlabeled and hand-labeled data, respectively. The red triangles represent the AI-generated labels

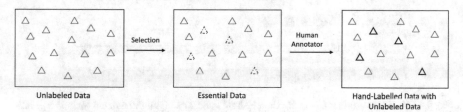

Fig. 4.2 Active (semi-supervised) learning reduces the total labeling workload by selecting only essential data to label. The dotted and solid black triangles represent the unlabeled and hand-labeled data, respectively. The dashed-dotted triangles represent the selected essential data to be labeled

Attacks can also target the vulnerabilities of these algorithms and mechanisms. For example, in active learning, an adversary may be able to introduce instances that appear appealing to the selection algorithm but have little impact on classification accuracy [46]. Therefore, beyond cognitive reliability methods, cognitive security methods aware of those algorithm-targeted attacks should be included in the future to mitigate labeling errors caused by inattention.

4.1.1.2 Human Users and Phishing

Two types of attention vulnerabilities can make human users the unwitting victims of phishing. On the one hand, careless users fail to notice many of the phishing indicators shown in Fig. 4.3. Phishers can intentionally exploit inattention to hide phishing indicators such as spelling errors. For example, at first glance, users cannot distinguish the spoof email address "paypa1@mail.paypal.com" from the authentic one "pay-pal@mail.paypal.com" while a guided close look reveals that the lowercase letter "l" is replaced by the number "1" and the capital letter "I". On the other hand, humans without vision defects can fail to perceive an obvious stimulus in plain sight, if they are focusing on other tasks and the stimulus is unexpected, known as *inattentional blindness* [42]. Take phishing email as an example, users

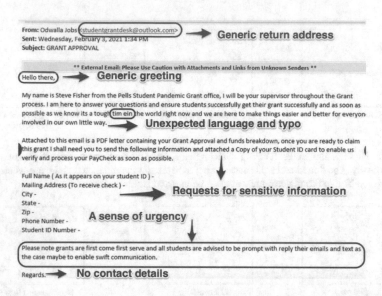

From: Odwalla Jobs <studentgrantdesk@outlook.com> → **Generic return address**
Sent: Wednesday, February 3, 2021 1:34 PM
Subject: GRANT APPROVAL

** External Email: Please Use Caution with Attachments and Links from Unknown Senders **

Hello there, → **Generic greeting**

My name is Steve Fisher from the Pells Student Pandemic Grant office, I will be your supervisor throughout the Grant
process. I am here to answer your questions and ensure students successfully get their grant successfully and as soon as
possible as we know its a tough tim ein the world right now and we are here to make things easier and better for everyon
involved in our own little way. → **Unexpected language and typo**

Attached to this email is a PDF letter containing your Grant Approval and funds breakdown, once you are ready to claim
this grant I shall need you to send the following information and attached a Copy of your Student ID card to enable us
verify and process your PayCheck as soon as possible.

Full Name (As it appears on your student ID) -
Mailing Address (To receive check) -
City -
State -   → **Requests for sensitive information**
Zip -
Phone Number -   **A sense of urgency**
Student ID Number -

Please note grants are first come first serve and all students are advised to be prompt with reply their emails and text as
the case maybe to enable swift communication.

Regards. → **No contact details**

Fig. 4.3 An example phishing email. The phishing indicators highlighted in red include a generic
return address, a generic greeting, unexpected language, a request for personal information, a sense
of urgency, and no contact details provided [71]

focusing on the main content can fail to perceive unloaded logos in a phishing email
[3].

Attention enhancement mechanisms, including highlights of contents [40, 83],
warnings of suspicious hyperlinks and attachments [1, 11], and anti-phishing educational messages [72], have been developed *empirically* to mitigate the phisher's
adversarial exploitation of the above human attention vulnerabilities.

To better design attention enhancement mechanisms, we need an *analytical*
understanding of human attention, which requires the collection and analysis of
high-quality human data. Thus, on the one hand, researchers have incorporated
biosensors, including eye trackers and electroencephalogram (EEG) devices, for
data collection. On the other hand, system-scientific methods, including machine
learning, have been increasingly incorporated to process the human data to improve
the design of attention enhancement mechanisms. In particular, researchers have
investigated the users' gaze behaviors and attention when reading Uniform Resource
Locators (URLs) [61], phishing websites [48], and phishing emails [9, 44, 83]. These
works illustrate the users' visual processing of phishing contents [44, 48, 56, 61]
and the effects of visual aids [83]. The authors in [48] further establish correlations
between eye movements and phishing identification to estimate the likelihood that
users may fall victim to phishing attacks.

Most of the existing cognitive security methods provide an *offline* solution by
analyzing a pre-collected human data set. We refer the reader to the ADVERT
framework in Chap. 5 for an *online* solution where RL is applied to change visual-
aid adaptively to enhance attention in real time.

4.1.1.3 Human Operators and Alert Fatigue

In the age of "infobesity" with terabytes of unprocessed data or manipulated information, many alerts are false. It is estimated that 72–99% of all clinical alarms [69] and nearly half of all cybersecurity alerts [79] are false, respectively. The overwhelming volume of false alarms leads to the serious problem of alert fatigue. According to the Ponemon Institute research report [41], organizations spend nearly 21,000 h each year analyzing false alarms, which costs organizations an average of $1.27 million per year.

Since real-time monitoring and alert inspection belong to tasks of long duration and frequent interference, Sustained Attention (SA) and Divided Attention (DA) play important roles. Besides a psychological understanding of attention vulnerabilities concerning SA and DA, we can also explain the cause of alert fatigue from an economic perspective. As described in *rational inattention theory* [74], humans pay less attention when the attention cost outweighs the benefit of information resulting from paying attention. Since the high percentage of false alarms reduces the average benefit of alert monitoring and inspection, humans tend to ignore alerts unintentionally or are less sensitive to true-positive alerts.

The existing methods mitigate alert fatigue mainly through the following three perspectives. First, alert management techniques, including alert aggregation and correlation [35, 66], can reorganize alerts of similar events to reduce the total number of alerts. Second, system-scientific methods, including machine learning and data mining [58, 81], have been applied to reduce the percentage of false alarms. Third, the researchers have investigated the presentation forms of alerts to reduce the cognitive load when processing the alerts [26], and alert fatigue metrics have been suggested in [30].

The first two classes of methods offer *technical* solutions to manage alerts and improve the accuracy of alerts, while the third class offers empirical *human* solutions to tailor the alert processing to human attention limitation. There is a need for a *human-technical* solution that can quantitatively and holistically manage alerts and human attention. Moreover, the existing methods focus on issues of cognitive reliability defined in Sect. 1.2.5.1. Since humans have limited capability to sustain attention and attend to multiple tasks simultaneously, IDoS attacks in Sect. 1.2.4 can intentionally deplete attention resources to exploit such attention vulnerabilities. To overcome these two challenges, we refer the readers to the RADAMS framework in Chap. 5 as an example of cognitive security methods, where RL is applied for resilient and adaptive alert and attention management against IDoS attacks.

4.1.2 Subjective Risk Perception

Many experiments and phenomena have shown that humans perceive risk subjectively. As a quantitative framework of human decisions under risk and uncertainty,

CPT in Sect. 2.1.2 has been incorporated in many works [28, 57, 68, 90] to enhance the security and efficiency of CPS.

Besides CPT, researchers have found other factors that affect human risk perception. For example, Cox et al. [9] shows that people believe they are less likely than others to engage in actions that pose a threat to their cyber security, particularly because they rely less on base rate information when predicting their own behavior compared to others' behavior. The authors in [36] list the 24 dimensions of cyber risk perception in different online environments from 25 articles. We select five of them below as an example. Other factors include newness, severity of consequence, and perceived benefit.

- **Voluntariness**: less voluntary exposure to a cyber threat leads to a higher risk perception.
- **Immediacy of Risk Consequences**: a greater perceived immediacy of cyber risks leads to a higher risk perception.
- **Knowledge to Exposed**: more familiarity with the cyber risk leads to lower risk perception.
- **Knowledge to Science/Experts**: a firmer belief that cyber risks are known to experts leads to lower risk perception.
- **Controllability**: a firmer belief that cyber risks are controllable leads to lower risk perception.

Attacks that understand these human perception patterns can craft their attacks accordingly. For example, they can inject different reference points and base information to make risky behaviors look safe, thus encouraging risky behaviors. All 24 dimensions of cyber risk perception described in [36] provide possibilities for adversarial exploitation, and thus cognitive security methods are required to be developed from all these perspectives.

4.1.3   Vulnerabilities of Reasoning and Decision Making

Morgenstern and Von Neumann establish modern decision theory based on Expected Utility Theory (EUT) on which we have elaborated in Sect. 2.1.1. However, human rationality is limited by the tractability of the problem, the cognitive limitations of the mind, and the time available to make decisions. Thus, humans pursue bounded rationality within their capacity rather than perfect rationality, as pointed out by Simon [73] in 1957. Simon proposes to replace the optimization problem of maximizing expected utility with a simpler decision criterion called satisficing; i.e., humans stop finding the global optimal solution once they find one that meets or exceeds their aspiration level.

Cognitive attacks can exploit the bounded rationality of human users, operators, and administrators. Recognizing the bounded rationality of human decision-makers leads to two possible classes of cognitive security methods. On the one hand, we can reactively build strategy upon bounded rationality models to better manage risks

[8], uncertainty [76] and attacks [88]. On the other hand, since human attackers can also be prone to bounded rationality, we can proactively learn and counteract the attackers' behaviors that are restricted by bounded rationality [95].

In the following subsections, we briefly introduce some system-scientific models of bounded rationality for single-agent and multi-agent decisions and list their applications in HCPSs. We refer the readers to [64] for more bounded rationality models. Besides the notations in Chap. 2, we define the feasible action set as $\mathcal{A}$.

4.1.3.1 Epsilon-Rationality

In EUT, the agent aims to find an action $a \in \mathcal{A}$ to maximize the expected utility. Denote the expected utility under action a as $U(a)$, maximized expected utility as U^*, and $\epsilon \in \mathbb{R}^{0+}$ as the tolerance threshold of the agent. Then, following the satisficing criteria, the agent can accept any action as long as it brings utility larger than $U^* - \epsilon$, i.e.,

$$U(a) \geq U^* - \epsilon. \tag{4.1}$$

For games, we can generalize the NE in Definition 2.3 to the following ϵ-NE in Definition 4.1.

Definition 4.1 (ϵ-Nash Equilibrium (NE)) For a given $\epsilon \in \mathbb{R}^{0+}$, the set of N players' policies $\sigma^{1:I,*} \in \Delta\mathcal{A}^{1:I}$ comprises a mixed-strategy ϵ-NE if

$$v^i(\sigma^{i,*}, \sigma^{-i,*}) \geq v^i(\sigma^i, \sigma^{-i,*}) - \epsilon, \forall \sigma^i \in \Delta\mathcal{A}^i, \forall i \in \mathcal{I}. \tag{4.2}$$

4.1.3.2 Softmax and Quantal Response

In EUT, the optimal action $a^* \in \mathcal{A}$ is deterministic, i.e.,

$$a^* = arg \max_{a \in \mathcal{A}} U(a). \tag{4.3}$$

However, humans' choices may not always be deterministic and optimal. Suppose the action set $\mathcal{A}$ contains M feasible actions. Softmax model with parameter $\beta \in \mathbb{R}$ assumes that humans can choose any feasible action $a_m \in \mathcal{A}, m \in \{1, 2, \cdots, M\}$, with a probability $p_m \in [0, 1]$, where

$$p_m = \frac{e^{-\beta U(a_m)}}{\sum_{m=1}^{M} e^{-\beta U(a_m)}}. \tag{4.4}$$

We can extend the softmax decision to formulate the Quantal Response Equilibrium (QRE) in game theory. Logit equilibrium in Definition 4.2 is the most common specification of QRE. Suppose the action set $\mathcal{A}^i$ of player $i, i \in I$, contains M^i feasible actions.

Definition 4.2 (Logit Equilibrium (LQRE)) In a logit equilibrium, each player $i \in I$ chooses the j-th action $a_j^i \in \mathcal{A}^i$ with probability

$$\sigma^i(a_j^i) = \frac{e^{-\beta U_j^i(\sigma^1, \cdots, \sigma^I)}}{\sum_{k=1}^{M^i} e^{-\beta U_k^i(\sigma^1, \cdots, \sigma^I)}}, \, j \in \{1, 2, \cdots, M^i\}, \qquad (4.5)$$

where $U_j^i(\sigma^1, \cdots, \sigma^I))$ is the expected utility to player i of choosing action a_j^i when player $l \in I$ are playing according to the probability distribution σ^l.

Many works, e.g., [15, 19, 32], have adopted LQRE for the security of HCPSs.

4.1.3.3 Quantum Models

Quantum theory provides a new formalism for constructing probabilistic and dynamic systems, which has been applied to explain human decision-making due to the following five reasons [7].

- Judgments are based on indefinite states (i.e., superposition states). Compared to cognitive and decision sciences that model the cognitive system as a particle, the quantum theory provides a wave perspective by modeling the cognitive system as a wave moving across time over the state space until a decision is made.
- Judgments create rather than record. Taking a measurement of a human decision system (e.g., applying biosensors and asking questions) creates rather than records a property of the system (e.g., leading the person to form an idea).
- Judgments disturb each other, introducing uncertainty. The order of questioning can influence human decisions and introduce uncertainty.
- Judgments do not always obey classical logic and the *principle of unicity*. Classical logic and probability theory can be too restrictive to explain human judgments and decisions.
- Cognitive phenomena may not be decomposable. We may not be able to adopt a reductionist view where phenomena can be analyzed by considering their different components separately and then synthesizing the results obtained.

Many social and psychological experiments have produced contradictory results that classical cognition and decision theories are unable to explain. For example, Tversky and Shafir [77] discovers the *disjunction effect*, which contradicts the *sure thing principle* [38]. In particular, experiments have shown that even if a person prefers choice A under all conditions, he may not still prefer it when he is uncertain about the current condition. Therefore, quantum theory can be a promising direction to model human decision-making and cognition.

4.1.3.4 Level-k Reasoning

In a multi-agent environment, the outcome depends on all players' actions. Therefore, when making decisions, each agent needs to deduce the other's thoughts and, further, how others think about his decision-making strategy. Therefore, each agent needs to form a hierarchy of beliefs about others' beliefs.

Level-k theory characterizes human bounded rationality by the "depth" of their strategic thought. It starts with a non-rational level-0 player who chooses actions (usually randomly) while ignoring the actions of other players. Then, a level-k (or depth-k) player chooses his actions based on the assumption that all other players are level-$(k - 1)$ thinkers. For example, the Keynesian beauty contest [33] asks players to choose a number from the range 1–100 that is closest to the average of all participants' guesses. Then, a level-0 player chooses a random number in [0, 100], and a level-1 player thinking all players are level-0 chooses number 50, i.e., the average of level-0 players' choices. Level-2 players think that all other players are level-1 and chooses 50, and the average will be 25. Thus, level-2 players choose 25. The same reasoning repeats for higher-level players.

Level-k reasoning provides a good description of bounded rationality and belief hierarchy, and has been adopted to enhance HCPS security (e.g., [13, 31, 67]).

4.2 Acquired Vulnerabilities

The formulation of human cognition spans at least three different time scales: *slow*, for the billion years in which our brains have evolved; *fast*, for the fleeting weeks and months of infancy and childhood; and *in between*, the centuries of growth of our ideas through history [47]. The development of mind, the growth of ideas, and the evolution of the brain over years, centuries, and billions of years lead to the unique features of human cognition and the innate vulnerabilities described in Sect. 4.1.

Compared to innate vulnerabilities, acquired vulnerabilities, including two types of information-related vulnerabilities in Sect. 4.2.1 and incentive-related vulnerabilities in Sect. 4.2.2, can be mitigated by security training, education, and incentive programs.

4.2.1 Lack of Security Information and Knowledge

Knowing the risk is an indispensable precondition to averting it. Human users and operators who lack security knowledge can make their organizations vulnerable to attacks. It is estimated that 88% of employees lack the awareness needed to prevent common cyber incidents [5]. According to [27], 56% insider-driven incidents resulted from negligence, which leads to an annualized cost of 6.6 million dollars.

Lack of security awareness can also lead to improper trust and make humans the victims of Social Engineering (SE).

Training and awareness programs are critical for reducing employees' complacency in risky behaviors, as well as their erroneous trust in unsolicited emails and SE hackers. Besides regular classes, these programs can transfer security knowledge more actively and effectively through discussions, case studies, and education games [86]. The authors in [37] have summarized the most frequently used theories to understand security awareness. They are the Theory of Reasoned Action (TRA), Theory of Planned Behavior (TPB), General Deterrence Theory (GDT), Protection Motivation Theory (PMT), Technology Acceptance Model (TAM), Social Cognitive Theory (SCT), Constructivism, and Social Leaning Theory (SLT).

Lack of security awareness is not the only information-related vulnerability. As shown in Fig. 4.4, besides security knowledge that maps from security states to security decisions, information is also needed as an input to know the current situation for decision-making. Human operators with high security awareness may still make errors due to the following three difficulties of collecting, correlating, and analyzing information in HCPSs, which is referred to as a Type-1 information-related vulnerability.

- First, the large-scale integration of heterogeneous components in an HCPS leads to piecemeal information that can be hard to obtain.

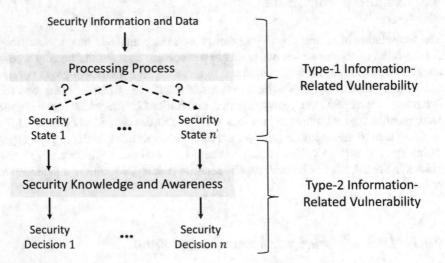

Fig. 4.4 The relationship between security information and security awareness. Security knowledge enables humans to take appropriate security decisions based on different security states. Security information provides input for humans to determine the current security state. Type-1 information-related vulnerability results from the difficulty of collecting, correlating, and analyzing information and data in an HCPS, while Type-2 vulnerability results from a lack of security awareness to use the information

- Second, the complexity of the HCPS architecture, procedures, and protocol has led to uncertainty and made it challenging to correlate and analyze collected data.
- Third, the presence of attacks can reduce the information quality by introducing noise and delaying the information acquisition.

Cognitive security methods have been developed to enhance the acquisition, sharing, and processing of security information and data, even under attacks. Acquisition [10] focuses on collecting security information from multiple sources and at different levels, while sharing [6, 65] encourages information exchanges between different agents. Finally, processing [17, 18] aims to abstract high-level system information from device-level raw data and estimate the current security state. Despite the above efforts, we may still face the challenge of incomplete and asymmetric information in HCPSs, especially when adversarial deception is introduced. We refer the readers to the discussion in Sect. 4.3 for game-theoretic models of incomplete information and deception in HCPSs.

4.2.2 Misaligned Incentive and Incompliance

In comparison to the two types of information-related vulnerabilities in Sect. 4.2.1, the agent now has all of the necessary information to act appropriately and understands the information correctly. However, he acts inappropriately because of his misaligned incentives. Most employees understand but do not follow the security rules if they are inconsistent with their incentives. For example, an employee who needs to finish an urgent report chooses to connect to a public airport WiFi, although the security rule states that the computer used to process the report should not connect to an untrusted network. Attackers can exacerbate the incompliance of human employees and turn self-interested employees into malicious ones to induce intentional insider threats. The adversarial exploitation of the misaligned incentives makes such cognitive attacks more targeted and easier to sustain.

There is rich literature on designing incentive mechanisms [49, 89, 94] to tilt the misaligned incentives. The majority of these methods aim to change incentives by reward or punishment, referred to as the *positive* and *negative* incentives in Moore et al. [49], respectively. According to McGregor [45], *Theory X* treats humans as a reactive machine where the incentives are external and indirectly come from the environment, while *Theory Y* treats humans as an active system where the incentives are internal and directly come from accomplishing the task itself. Although Theory X may better fit non-technical departments where tasks are less fulfilling, more and more evidence has emphasized the benefit of Theory Y. Besides the monetary rewards, humans may be better incentivized through a sense of achievement and belonging as well as an encompassing culture.

Besides reward and punishment, recent research has shown the potential of *information design* to develop compliance policies. Compared to the classical design of payment and allocation rules, information design provides an affordable, scalable, and complementary way to change agents' beliefs and achieve compliance. In recent works [16, 23, 25], the defender keeps their strategies *covert* to create information asymmetry and influence the agents' reasoning. For example, a defender with different assets can develop different defense schemes and strategically select one to implement. Since the agents do not know the defender's asset and the selection strategy, they may deduce the asset based on the evidence and revise their actions accordingly. On the other hand, ZETAR in [24] implements a *transparent* and *overt* recommendation strategy to align insiders' incentives, and the authors in [22] further develop a holistic framework to jointly design information and reward. In these works, the recommendation strategy is designed to be aligned with the agents' incentives, which is verifiable as it is overt. Thus, the agents are willing to follow the recommendation, and the defender can select the recommendation to his advantage.

4.3 Discussions

There are many other cognitive vulnerabilities exploitable by attacks that are out of the scope of this book, including vulnerabilities of trust, emotions, social conformity, and culture. Vulnerabilities of trust and emotions are related to ToM in Sect. 3.3.2 and the Type-1 information-related vulnerability in Sect. 4.2.1. SE attackers with a high-level ToM can exploit the trust and emotions of human users and operators [12] to distort the information processing process in Fig. 4.4. Hypergames [4] and Bayesian games [14] are two classical game models to characterize the asymmetric information, misperceptions, and deception in HCPSs. Dynamic hypergames (e.g., [39, 82]) and dynamic Bayesian games [20, 21, 23, 25] have been further developed to capture the multi-stage and multi-phase features of the APTs [62, 92]. In particular, signaling games [52, 55], one-sided information games [16], and Bayesian persuasions [29] have been used to quantify the evolution of trust in the context of insider threats [22, 24], autonomous systems [84, 85], medical devices [53], Internet of Things [54], and critical infrastructures [63].

Beyond these works, psychological game theory further incorporates personality (e.g., kindness [60]) and emotions (e.g., guiltiness [2]), and it can be used to model vulnerabilities of trust and emotions in HCPSs. Attacks can also exploit social and cultural vulnerabilities, including information cascade [91], herding [87], and cultural biases [34], to affect human behaviors and further compromise the security of HCPSs. Individual, interpersonal, and social vulnerabilities are interdependent. Individuals determine the interpersonal and social dynamics, while the social interactions among different types of individuals influence the evolution of cooperation between individuals and their trust.[2]

---

[2] An online game of trust evolution can be found at https://ncase.me/trust/.

References

1. Akhawe D, Felt AP (2013) Alice in warningland: a large-scale field study of browser security warning effectiveness. In: 22nd USENIX security symposium (USENIX Security 13), pp 257–272
2. Battigalli P, Dufwenberg M (2007) Guilt in games. Am Econ Rev 97(2):170–176
3. Baxter I (2020) Fake login attack evades logo detection. https://ironscales.com/blog/fake-login-attack-evades-logo-detection
4. Bennett PG (1980) Hypergames: developing a model of conflict. Futures 12(6):489–507
5. Bothell W (2016) 88% of employees lack the awareness needed to prevent common cyber incidents. https://www.businesswire.com/news/home/20161026005371/en/Report-88-of-Employees-Lack-the-Awareness-Needed-to-Prevent-Common-Cyber-Incidents
6. Brown S, Gommers J, Serrano O (2015) From cyber security information sharing to threat management. In: Proceedings of the 2nd ACM workshop on information sharing and collaborative security, pp 43–49
7. Busemeyer JR, Bruza PD (2012) Quantum models of cognition and decision. Cambridge University Press
8. Chen J, Zhu Q (2019) Interdependent strategic security risk management with bounded rationality in the internet of things. IEEE Trans Inf Forens Secur 14(11):2958–2971
9. Cox EB, Zhu Q, Balcetis E (2020) Stuck on a phishing lure: differential use of base rates in self and social judgments of susceptibility to cyber risk. Compr Results Soc Psychol 4(1):25–52
10. Cruz T, Rosa L, Proença J, Maglaras L, Aubigny M, Lev L, Jiang J, Simões P (2016) A cybersecurity detection framework for supervisory control and data acquisition systems. IEEE Trans Ind Inf 12(6):2236–2246
11. Egelman S, Cranor LF, Hong J (2008) You've been warned: an empirical study of the effectiveness of web browser phishing warnings. In: Proceedings of the SIGCHI conference on human factors in computing systems, pp 1065–1074
12. Hadnagy C (2010) Social engineering: the art of human hacking. John Wiley & Sons
13. Hamman S, Hopkinson K, McCarty L (2017) Applying behavioral game theory to cyber-physical systems protection planning. In: Cyber-physical systems. Elsevier, pp 251–264
14. Harsanyi JC (1968) Games with incomplete information played by "Bayesian" players part II. Bayesian equilibrium points. Manag Sci 14(5):320–334
15. Hasan K, Shetty S, Islam T, Ahmed I (2022) Predictive cyber defense remediation against advanced persistent threat in cyber-physical systems. In: 2022 International conference on computer communications and networks (ICCCN). IEEE, pp 1–10
16. Horák K, Bošanský B, Tomášek P, Kiekintveld C, Kamhoua C (2019) Optimizing honeypot strategies against dynamic lateral movement using partially observable stochastic games. Comput Secur 87. https://doi.org/10.1016/j.cose.2019.101579
17. Hu Q, Fooladivanda D, Chang YH, Tomlin CJ (2017) Secure state estimation and control for cyber security of the nonlinear power systems. IEEE Trans Control Netw Syst 5(3):1310–1321
18. Hu L, Wang Z, Han QL, Liu X (2018) State estimation under false data injection attacks: security analysis and system protection. Automatica 87:176–183
19. Hu H, Liu Y, Chen C, Zhang H, Liu Y (2020) Optimal decision making approach for cyber security defense using evolutionary game. IEEE Trans Netw Serv Manag 17(3):1683–1700
20. Huang L, Zhu Q (2018) Analysis and computation of adaptive defense strategies against advanced persistent threats for cyber-physical systems. In: International conference on decision and game theory for security. Springer, Cham, pp 205–226
21. Huang L, Zhu Q (2019) Adaptive strategic cyber defense for advanced persistent threats in critical infrastructure networks. In: ACM SIGMETRICS performance evaluation review, vol 46. ACM, pp 52–56
22. Huang L, Zhu Q (2021) Duplicity games for deception design with an application to insider threat mitigation. IEEE Trans Inf Forens Secur 16:4843–4856

23. Huang L, Zhu Q (2021) A dynamic game framework for rational and persistent robot deception with an application to deceptive pursuit-evasion. IEEE Trans Autom Sci Eng 19:2918
24. Huang L, Zhu Q (2022) Zetar: modeling and computational design of strategic and adaptive compliance policies. Preprint. arXiv:220402294. https://doi.org/10.48550/ARXIV.2204.02294
25. Huang Y, Chen J, Huang L, Zhu Q (2020) Dynamic games for secure and resilient control system design. Natl Sci Rev 7(7):1125–1141
26. Hussain MI, Reynolds TL, Zheng K (2019) Medication safety alert fatigue may be reduced via interaction design and clinical role tailoring: a systematic review. J Am Med Inf Assoc 26(10):1141–1149
27. Institute P (2022) 2022 ponemon cost of insider threats global report. https://www.proofpoint.com/us/resources/threat-reports/cost-of-insider-threats
28. Jhala K, Natarajan B, Pahwa A (2018) Prospect theory-based active consumer behavior under variable electricity pricing. IEEE Trans Smart Grid 10(3):2809–2819
29. Kamenica E, Gentzkow M (2011) Bayesian persuasion. Am Econ Rev 101(6):2590–2615
30. Kane-Gill SL, O'Connor MF, Rothschild JM, Selby NM, McLean B, Bonafide CP, Cvach MM, Hu X, Konkani A, Pelter MM, et al (2017) Technologic distractions (part 1): summary of approaches to manage alert quantity with intent to reduce alert fatigue and suggestions for alert fatigue metrics. Crit Care Med 45(9):1481–1488
31. Kanellopoulos A, Vamvoudakis KG (2019) Non-equilibrium dynamic games and cyber–physical security: a cognitive hierarchy approach. Syst Control Lett 125:59–66
32. Kantzavelou I, Katsikas S (2010) A game-based intrusion detection mechanism to confront internal attackers. Comput Secur 29(8):859–874
33. Keynes JM (1937) The general theory of employment. Q J Econ 51(2):209–223
34. King ZM, Henshel DS, Flora L, Cains MG, Hoffman B, Sample C (2018) Characterizing and measuring maliciousness for cybersecurity risk assessment. Front Psychol 9:39
35. Landauer M, Skopik F, Wurzenberger M, Rauber A (2022) Dealing with security alert flooding: using machine learning for domain-independent alert aggregation. ACM Trans Privacy Secur 25(3):1–36
36. Larsen MH, Lund MS (2021) A maritime perspective on cyber risk perception: a systematic literature review. IEEE Access 9:144895
37. Lebek B, Uffen J, Neumann M, Hohler B, Breitner MH (2014) Information security awareness and behavior: a theory-based literature review. Manag Res Rev 37:1049
38. Leonard JS, et al (1954) The foundations of statistics. John Wiley, New York, pp 188–190
39. Li L, Ma H, Kulkarni AN, Fu J (2023) Dynamic hypergames for synthesis of deceptive strategies with temporal logic objectives. IEEE Trans Autom Sci Eng 20(1):334–345. https://doi.org/10.1109/tase.2022.3150167
40. Lin E, Greenberg S, Trotter E, Ma D, Aycock J (2011) Does domain highlighting help people identify phishing sites? In: Proceedings of the SIGCHI conference on human factors in computing systems, pp 2075–2084
41. LLC PI (2015) The cost of malware containment. Tech. rep.
42. Mack A, Rock I (1998) Inattentional blindness: perception without attention. Visual Attention 8:55–76
43. Mall S (2022) Are label errors imperative? Is confident learning useful? https://towardsdatascience.com/confident-learning-err-did-you-say-your-data-is-clean-ef2597903328
44. McAlaney J, Hills PJ (2020) Understanding phishing email processing and perceived trustworthiness through eye tracking. Front Psychol 11:1756
45. McGregor D (1960) Theory X and theory Y. Organ Theory 358(374):5
46. Miller B, Kantchelian A, Afroz S, Bachwani R, Dauber E, Huang L, Tschantz MC, Joseph AD, Tygar JD (2014) Adversarial active learning. In: Proceedings of the 2014 workshop on artificial intelligent and security workshop, pp 3–14
47. Minsky M (1988) Society of mind. Simon and Schuster

48. Miyamoto D, Blanc G, Kadobayashi Y (2015) Eye can tell: on the correlation between eye movement and phishing identification. In: Int. Conf. on neural information processing. Springer, pp 223–232
49. Moore A, Savinda J, Monaco E, Moyes J, Rousseau D, Perl S, Cowley J, Collins M, Cassidy T, VanHoudnos N, Buttles P, Bauer D, Parshall A (2016) The critical role of positive incentives for reducing insider threats. Tech. Rep. CMU/SEI-2016-TR-014, Software Engineering Institute, Carnegie Mellon University, Pittsburgh, PA
50. Northcutt C, Jiang L, Chuang I (2021) Confident learning: estimating uncertainty in dataset labels. J Artif Intell Res 70:1373–1411
51. Northcutt CG, Athalye A, Mueller J (2021) Pervasive label errors in test sets destabilize machine learning benchmarks. Preprint. arXiv:210314749
52. Pawlick J, Zhu Q (2017) Proactive defense against physical denial of service attacks using poisson signaling games. In: International conference on decision and game theory for security. Springer, pp 336–356
53. Pawlick J, Zhu Q (2017) Strategic trust in cloud-enabled cyber-physical systems with an application to glucose control. IEEE Trans Inf Forens Secur 12(12):2906–2919
54. Pawlick J, Chen J, Zhu Q (2018) istrict: an interdependent strategic trust mechanism for the cloud-enabled internet of controlled things. IEEE Trans Inf Forens Secur 14(6):1654–1669
55. Pawlick J, Colbert E, Zhu Q (2018) Modeling and analysis of leaky deception using signaling games with evidence. IEEE Trans Inf Forens Secur 14(7):1871–1886
56. Pfeffel K, Ulsamer P, Müller N (2019) Where the user does look when reading phishing mails–an eye-tracking study. In: Int. Conf. on human-computer interaction. Springer, pp 277–287
57. Pfleeger SL, Caputo DD (2012) Leveraging behavioral science to mitigate cyber security risk. Comput Secur 31(4):597–611
58. Pietraszek T, Tanner A (2005) Data mining and machine learning—towards reducing false positives in intrusion detection. Inf Secur Technical Rep 10(3):169–183
59. Quinn AJ, Bederson BB (2011) Human computation: a survey and taxonomy of a growing field. In: Proceedings of the SIGCHI conference on human factors in computing systems, pp 1403–1412
60. Rabin M (1993) Incorporating fairness into game theory and economics. Am Econ Rev 83:1281–1302
61. Ramkumar N, Kothari V, Mills C, Koppel R, Blythe J, Smith S, Kun AL (2020) Eyes on URLs: relating visual behavior to safety decisions. In: ACM symposium on eye tracking research and applications, pp 1–10
62. Rass S, Alshawish A, Abid MA, Schauer S, Zhu Q, De Meer H (2017) Physical intrusion games—optimizing surveillance by simulation and game theory. IEEE Access 5:8394–8407
63. Rass S, Schauer S, König S, Zhu Q (2020) Cyber-security in critical infrastructures. Springer
64. Rubinstein A (1998) Modeling bounded rationality. MIT Press
65. Rutkowski A, Kadobayashi Y, Furey I, Rajnovic D, Martin R, Takahashi T, Schultz C, Reid G, Schudel G, Hird M, et al (2010) Cybex: the cybersecurity information exchange framework (x. 1500). ACM SIGCOMM Comput Commun Rev 40(5):59–64
66. Salah S, Maciá-Fernández G, Díaz-Verdejo JE (2013) A model-based survey of alert correlation techniques. Comput Netw 57(5):1289–1317
67. Sanjab A, Saad W (2016) On bounded rationality in cyber-physical systems security: game-theoretic analysis with application to smart grid protection. In: 2016 Joint workshop on cyber-physical security and resilience in smart grids (CPSR-SG). IEEE, pp 1–6
68. Sanjab A, Saad W, Başar T (2020) A game of drones: Cyber-physical security of time-critical UAV applications with cumulative prospect theory perceptions and valuations. IEEE Trans Commun 68(11):6990–7006
69. Sendelbach S, Funk M (2013) Alarm fatigue: a patient safety concern. AACN Adv Crit Care 24(4):378–386
70. Settles B (2012) Active learning. Synthesis lectures on artificial intelligence and machine learning. https://doi.org/10.1007/978-3-031-01560-1

71. Sharma L (2021) Phishing campaigns targeting students with pandemic & pell grant funds. https://wp.nyu.edu/itsecurity/2021/02/05/phishing-campaigns-targeting-students-with-pandemic-pell-grant-funds/
72. Sheng S, Holbrook M, Kumaraguru P, Cranor LF, Downs J (2010) Who falls for phish? A demographic analysis of phishing susceptibility and effectiveness of interventions. In: Proceedings of the SIGCHI conference on human factors in computing systems, pp 373–382
73. Simon HA (1957) A behavioral model of rational choice. In: Models of man, social and rational: mathematical essays on rational human behavior in a social setting. Wiley, pp 241–260
74. Sims CA (2003) Implications of rational inattention. J Monetary Econ 50(3):665–690
75. Technology K (2022) Things that can go wrong during annotation and how to avoid them. https://kili-technology.com/blog/things-that-can-go-wrong-during-annotation-and-how-to-avoid-them#164
76. Thakoor O, Jabbari S, Aggarwal P, Gonzalez C, Tambe M, Vayanos P (2020) Exploiting bounded rationality in risk-based cyber camouflage games. In: International conference on decision and game theory for security. Springer, pp 103–124
77. Tversky A, Shafir E (1992) The disjunction effect in choice under uncertainty. Psychol Sci 3(5):305–310
78. van der Wal D, Jhun I, Laklouk I, Nirschl J, Richer L, Rojansky R, Theparee T, Wheeler J, Sander J, Feng F, et al (2021) Biological data annotation via a human-augmenting ai-based labeling system. NPJ Digit Med 4(1):1–7
79. Vigliarolo B (2021) The number of false positive security alerts is staggering. here's what you can do to reduce yours. Tech. rep., https://www.techrepublic.com/article/the-number-of-false-positive-security-alerts-is-staggering-heres-what-you-can-do-to-reduce-yours/
80. Von Ahn L, Maurer B, McMillen C, Abraham D, Blum M (2008) recaptcha: Human-based character recognition via web security measures. Science 321(5895):1465–1468
81. Wagh SK, Pachghare VK, Kolhe SR (2013) Survey on intrusion detection system using machine learning techniques. Int J Comput Appl 78(16):30
82. Wan Z, Cho JH, Zhu M, Anwar AH, Kamhoua CA, Singh MP (2021) Foureye: defensive deception against advanced persistent threats via hypergame theory. IEEE Trans Netw Serv Manag 19(1):112–129
83. Xiong A, Proctor RW, Yang W, Li N (2017) Is domain highlighting actually helpful in identifying phishing web pages? Hum Factors 59(4):640–660
84. Xu Z, Zhu Q (2015) A cyber-physical game framework for secure and resilient multi-agent autonomous systems. In: 2015 54th IEEE conference on decision and control (CDC). IEEE, pp 5156–5161
85. Xu Z, Zhu Q (2016) Cross-layer secure cyber-physical control system design for networked 3d printers. In: 2016 American control conference (ACC). IEEE, pp 1191–1196
86. Yasin A, Liu L, Li T, Wang J, Zowghi D (2018) Design and preliminary evaluation of a cyber security requirements education game (SREG). Inf Softw Technol 95:179–200
87. Yousaf I, Ali S, Bouri E, Dutta A (2021) Herding on fundamental/nonfundamental information during the covid-19 outbreak and cyber-attacks: evidence from the cryptocurrency market. SAGE Open 11(3):21582440211029911
88. Zhang Y, Liu J (2019) Optimal decision-making approach for cyber security defense using game theory and intelligent learning. Secur Commun Netw 2019:1–16. https://doi.org/10.1155/2019/3038586
89. Zhang Y, Zhang H, Tang S, Zhong S (2016) Designing secure and dependable mobile sensing mechanisms with revenue guarantees. IEEE Trans Inf Forens Secur 11(1):100–113. https://doi.org/10.1109/TIFS.2015.2478739
90. Zhao M, Gao H, Wei G, Wei C, Guo Y (2022) Model for network security service provider selection with probabilistic uncertain linguistic TODIM method based on prospect theory. Technol Econ Devel Econ 28(3):638–654
91. Zhou F, Xu X, Trajcevski G, Zhang K (2021) A survey of information cascade analysis: Models, predictions, and recent advances. ACM Comput Surv (CSUR) 54(2):1–36

92. Zhu Q, Rass S (2018) On multi-phase and multi-stage game-theoretic modeling of advanced persistent threats. IEEE Access 6:13958–13971
93. Zhu X, Lafferty J, Ghahramani Z (2003) Combining active learning and semi-supervised learning using gaussian fields and harmonic functions. In: ICML 2003 workshop on the continuum from labeled to unlabeled data in machine learning and data mining, vol 3
94. Zhu Q, Fung C, Boutaba R, Basar T (2012) Guidex: a game-theoretic incentive-based mechanism for intrusion detection networks. IEEE J Sel Areas Commun 30(11):2220–2230
95. Zychowski A, Mańdziuk J (2021) Learning attacker's bounded rationality model in security games. In: International conference on neural information processing. Springer, pp 530–539

Chapter 5
ADVERT: Defending against Reactive Attention Attacks

Abstract Following the definition in Sect. 1.2.3.2, phishing can be a typical class of reactive attention attacks that exploit inattention to evade detection. This chapter proposes ADVERT, a *human-technical solution* that generates adaptive visual aids in real-time to prevent users from inadvertence and reduce their susceptibility to phishing attacks. Based on eye-tracking data, we extract *visual states* and *attention states* as system-level sufficient statistics to characterize the user's visual behaviors and attention status. By adopting a data-driven approach and two learning feedback of different time scales, this work lays out a theoretical foundation to *analyze*, *evaluate*, and particularly *modify* humans' attention processes while they vet and recognize phishing emails. We corroborate the *effectiveness*, *efficiency*, and *robustness* of ADVERT through a case study based on the data set collected from human subject experiments conducted at New York University. The results show that the visual aids can statistically increase the attention level and improve the accuracy of phishing recognition from 74.6% to a minimum of 86%. The meta-adaptation can further improve the accuracy to 91.5% (resp. 93.7%) in less than 3 (resp. 50) tuning stages.

Keywords Attention management · Phishing mitigation · Reinforcement learning · Bayesian optimization · Eye tracking · Reactive attention vulnerability

5.1 Introduction

Phishing is a Social Engineering (SE) method for the attacker to deliver a deceptive message designed to trick human victims into revealing sensitive information to the attacker, which violates the confidentiality of cognitive security as defined in Sect. 1.2.5.2.

According to [3], humans fall victim to phishing due to the following reasons: lack of security knowledge (e.g., www.ebay-members-security.com does not belong to www.ebay.com), visual deception (e.g., the legitimate hyperlink is an image that itself serves as a hyperlink to a malicious site), and lack of attention (e.g., careless users fail to notice the phishing indicators).

Following defense methods in Fig. 1.8, the existing phishing mitigation methods mainly fall into the categories of user training and cyber defense. The user training solution aims to train people to recognize phishing attempts and provide best practices to users. This solution is purely based on human behavior studies. The technical cyber defense solutions, including filtering, detection, and blacklisting, focus on creating a protection mechanism that reduces the chances of phishing emails reaching users. But the protection mechanism can fail when a human still seeks to open the phishing email or when a misdetected phishing email reaches an unmindful user.

Compared to these classical solutions that focus on humans and technologies disjointedly, we leverage the recent advances in data science and biosensor technology to develop human-technical solutions illustrated by the AI-powered enhancer in Fig. 1.8. The goal of such a human-technical solution is to design data-driven mechanisms that understand human responses (including eye-gaze locations, pupil size, and phishing judgment) and compensate for human vulnerabilities in real-time by changing visual aids adaptively.

In the following subsections, we illustrate the design of a human-technical solution called ADVERT[1] [5] to mitigate phishing by strategically enhancing the attention of human users. In particular, ADVERT leverages real-time eye-tracking data and phishing recognition results of users to design adaptive visual aids that can guide and sustain their attention to the right content of an email and consequently makes them less likely to fall victim to phishing. The design of the ADVERT contains two feedback loops for attention enhancement and phishing prevention at short and long time scales, respectively, as shown in Fig. 5.1.

The bottom part of Fig. 5.1 in blue illustrates the design of adaptive visual aids (e.g., highlighting, warnings, and educational messages) to engage human users in email vetting. First, when a human user reads emails and determines whether they are phishing or legitimate, a covert eye-tracking device can capture eye-gaze locations and pupil sizes in real time. Second, using the eye-tracking data, we abstract the email's Areas of Interest (AoIs), such as the title, hyperlinks, and attachments, and create a Visual State (VS) transition model to characterize the eye-gaze dynamics. Third, we develop system-level attention metrics to evaluate the user's attention level based on the VS transition trajectory. Then, we quantize the attention level to obtain the Attention State (AS) and develop adaptive learning algorithms to generate visual aids as feedback of the AS. The visual aids change the user's hidden cognitive states and lead to the set of eye-tracking data with different patterns of VS transition and AS, which then updates the design of visual aids and enhances attention iteratively.

The attention enhancement loop serves as a stepping-stone to achieving the ultimate goal of phishing prevention. The orange background in the top part of Fig. 5.1 illustrates how we tune the hyperparameters in the attention enhancement

---

[1] ADVERT is an acronym for ADaptive Visual aids for Efficient Real-time security-assistive Technology.

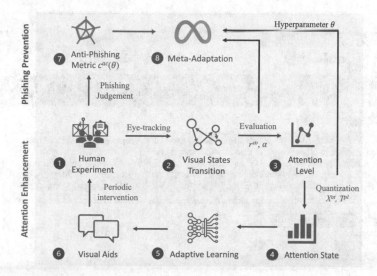

Fig. 5.1 The design diagram of ADVERT that provide a human-technical solution through eye-tracking data, visual aids, and learning techniques to counteract adversarial cyber deception. The adaptive learning loops of the attention enhancement mechanism and the phishing prevention mechanism are highlighted using blue and orange backgrounds, respectively. Since a user needs to persistently pay attention to an email to make a phishing judgment, the meta-adaptation feedback in orange updates less frequently than the feedback of attention enhancement in blue

loop to safeguard users from phishing emails. First, we create a metric to evaluate the user's accuracy in phishing recognition under the current attention enhancement mechanism. Then, we iteratively revise the hyperparameters to achieve the highest accuracy. Since the accuracy evaluation depends on the implementation of the entire attention enhancement loop, the evaluation is costly and time-consuming. Thus, we leverage Bayesian Optimization (BO) in Sect. 5.3.2 to propose an efficient meta-level tuning algorithm that improves the accuracy.

We elaborate on the two feedback loops of Fig. 5.1 in Sects. 5.2 and 5.3, respectively. Section 5.4 presents a case study of ADVERT for email vetting and phishing recognition.

5.2 Attention Enhancement Mechanism

As illustrated by Step 1 of Fig. 5.1, we consider a group of M human users who vet a list of N emails and classify them as phishing or legitimate. As a user $m \in \mathcal{M} := \{1, \cdots, M\}$ reads an email $n \in \mathcal{N} := \{1, \cdots, N\}$ on the screen for a duration of T_m^n, the eye-tracking device records the vertical and the horizontal coordinates of his eye gaze point in real-time. To compress the sensory outcomes and facilitate RL-driven attention enhancement solutions, we aggregate potential gaze locations (i.e., pixels

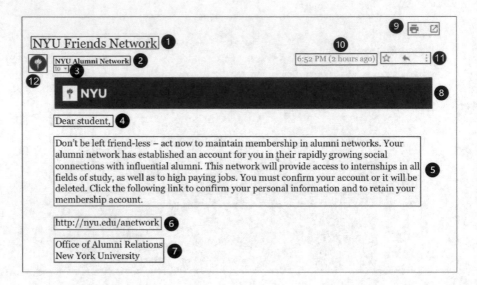

Fig. 5.2 A sample email with 12 AoIs. In sequence, they are the email's title, the sender's information, the receiver's information, the salutation, the main content, the URL, the sender's signature, the organization logo, the "print" and "share" buttons, the timestamp, the "bookmark" and "forward" buttons, and the sender's profile picture. The AoI partition in red boxes and their index numbers in black circles are invisible to users

on the screen) into a finite number of I non-overlapping Areas of Interest (AoIs) as shown in Fig. 5.2. We index each potential AoI by $i \in \mathcal{I} := \{1, 2, ..., I\}$.

We refer to all other areas in the email (e.g., blank areas) as the *uninformative area*. When the user's eyes move off the screen during the email vetting process, no coordinates of the gaze location are available. We refer to these off-screen areas as the *distraction area*.

5.2.1   Visual State Transition Model

As illustrated by Step 2 in Fig. 5.1, we establish the following transition model based on the AoI to which the user's gaze location belongs at different times. We define $\mathcal{S} := \{s^i\}_{i \in \mathcal{I}} \cup \{s^{ua}, s^{da}\}$ as the set of $I + 2$ *Visual States (VSs)*, where s^i represents the i-th AoI; s^{ua} represents the *uninformative area*; and s^{da} represents the *distraction area*. We provide an example transition map of these VSs in Fig. 5.3. The links represent the potential shifts of the gaze locations during the email reading process; e.g., a user can shift his focus from the title to the main content or the distraction area. We omit most links for illustration purposes; e.g., It is also possible for a user to regain attention to the AoIs from distraction or inadvertence.

We denote $s_t \in \mathcal{S}$ as the VS of user $m \in \mathcal{M}$ vetting email $n \in \mathcal{N}$ at time $t \in [0, T_m^n]$. In this work, we do not distinguish among human users concerning

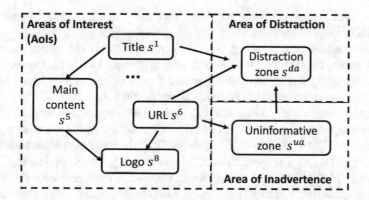

Fig. 5.3 Transitions among VSs in $\mathcal{S}$. The VS indices are consistent with the AoI indices in Fig. 5.2

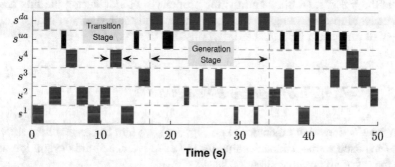

Fig. 5.4 An exemplary VS transition trajectory $[s_t]_{t \in [0, T_m^n]}$. The x-axis and the y-axis represent $T_m^n = 50$ s and $I + 2 = 6$ VSs, respectively. We denote VSs s^{da}, s^{ua}, and $\{s^i\}_{i \in I}$ in red, black, and blue, respectively. Each generation stage can contain different numbers of transition stages

their attention processes while they read different emails. Then, each user's gaze path during the interval $[0, T_m^n]$ can be characterized as the same stochastic process $[s_t]_{t \in [0, T_m^n]}$. The stochastic transition of the VSs divides the entire time interval $[0, T_m^n]$ into different *transition stages*. We visualize an exemplary VS transition trajectory $[s_t]_{t \in [0, T_m^n]}$ in Fig. 5.4 under $I = 4$ AoIs and $T_m^n = 50$ s. As denoted by the colored squares, 40 VSs arrive in sequence, which results in 40 discrete transition stages.

5.2.2 Feedback Visual-Aid Design

Proper visual aids can help guide and sustain the users' attention. Previous works have proposed different classes of visual aids to enhance phishing recognition.

These potential classes of visual aids construct the visual-aid library denoted as a finite set $\mathcal{A}$.

As illustrated by Step 6 in Fig. 5.1, different visual aids can affect the users' visual behaviors. In this paper, we focus on adapting visual aids to the human visual attention. We apply RL to learn the dynamic design of visual aids based on the real-time evaluation of the user's attention status detailed in Sect. 5.2.3.

The sequence of adaptive visual aids is generated with a period of length T^{pl}, and we refer to the time interval between every two visual aids as the *generation stage* indexed by $k \in \mathcal{K}_m^n := \{1, 2, \cdots, K_m^n\}$, where K_m^n is the maximum generation stage during $[0, T_m^n]$; i.e., $K_m^n T^{pl} \leq T_m^n$ and $(K_m^n + 1)T^{pl} \geq T_m^n$. Then, we denote $a_k \in \mathcal{A}$ as the visual aid at the k-th generation stage. Figure 5.4 illustrates how visual aids affect the transition of VSs in $K_m^n = 3$ generation stages divided by the two vertical dashed lines. In particular, during the second generation stage, an improper visual aid leads to more frequent transitions to the distraction area and also a longer sojourn time at the VS s^{da}. On the contrary, the proper visual aids during the first and the third generation stages engage the users and extend their attention spans, i.e., the amount of time spent on AoIs before a transition to s^{da} or s^{ua}.

5.2.3   Evaluation of Attention Status

From the VS transition trajectory (e.g., Fig. 5.4), we aim to construct the *Attention State (AS)* used as the feedback value for the adaptive visual-aid design. We define X as the set of all possible attention states.

5.2.3.1   Concentration Scores and Decay Rates

Both the gaze location and the gaze duration matter in the identification of phishing attacks. Therefore, we assign a *concentration score* $r^{co}(s) \in \mathbb{R}$ to characterize the sustained attention associated with VS $s \in S$. Since the amount of information that a user can extract from a VS $s \in S$ is limited, we use an exponential decay rate of $\alpha(s) \in \mathbb{R}^+$ to penalize the effect of concentration score as time elapses. Different VSs can have different concentration scores and decay rates. For example, the main content AoI (i.e., area 5 in Fig. 5.2) usually contains more information than other AoIs, and an extended attention span extracts more information (e.g., the substitution of letter 'l' into 'I') to identify the phishing email. Thus, the main content AoI turns to have a high concentration score and a low decay rate.

5.2.3.2   Cumulative Attention Level

We construct the metric for attention level illustrated by Step 3 in Fig. 5.1 as follows. Let $W_k \in \mathbb{Z}^+$ be the total number of transition stages contained in generation stage

$k \in \mathcal{K}_m^n$. Then, we define $t_k^{w_k}$, $w_k \in \{1, 2, \cdots, W_k\}$, as the duration of the w_k-th transition stage in the k-th generation stage. Take the gaze path in Fig. 5.4 as an example, the first generation stage contains $w_1 = 12$ transition stages and the first 7 transition stages last for a total of $\sum_{w_1=1}^{7} t_1^{w_1} = 10$ s. Based on the sets of scores associated with $s \in \mathcal{S}$, we compute the cumulative reward $u_k^{w_k}(s, t)$ at time t of the w_k-th transition stage in the k-th generation stage as $u_k^{w_k}(s, t) = \int_0^t r^{co}(s) e^{-\alpha(s)\tau} \cdot \mathbf{1}_{\{s=s^\tau\}} d\tau$, $0 \le t \le t_k^{w_k}$. At generation stage k, we define $\bar{w}_k^t$ as the latest transition stage before time t, i.e., $\sum_{w_k=1}^{\bar{w}_k^t} t_k^{w_k} \le t$ and $\sum_{w_k=1}^{\bar{w}_k^t+1} t_k^{w_k} > t$. Then, we define the user's *Cumulative Attention Level (CAL)* $v_k(t)$ over time interval $[(k-1)T^{pl}, t]$ at generation stage $k \in \mathcal{K}_m^n$ as the following cumulative reward

$$v_k(t) := \sum_{s \in \mathcal{S}} \sum_{w_k=1}^{\bar{w}_k^t} u_k^{w_k}(s, t), 0 \le t \le T^{pl}, \tag{5.1}$$

We visualize the CAL of $K_m^n = 3$ generation stages in Fig. 5.5 based on the gaze path in Fig. 5.4.

Since $v_k(t)$ is bounded for all $k \in \mathcal{K}_m^n, t \in [0, T^{pl}]$, we can quantize it into X finite values to construct the set $\mathcal{X}$ of the attention states illustrated by Step 4 in Fig. 5.1. We represent the quantized value of $v_k(t) \in \mathbb{R}$ as $v_k^{qu}(t) \in \mathcal{X}$ for all $k \in \mathcal{K}_m^n, t \subset [0, T^{pl}]$, and define the Average Attention Level (AAL) and Quantized Average Attention Level (QAAL) for each generation stage in Definition 5.1.

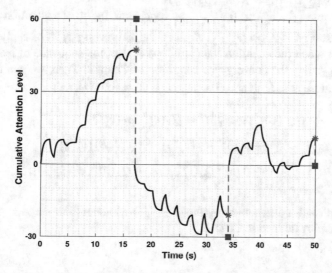

Fig. 5.5 The user's cumulative attention level $v_k(t - (k-1)T^{pl})$, $k \in \mathcal{K}_m^n, t \in [(k-1)T^{pl}, kT^{pl}]$, over $K_m^n = 3$ generation stages in $T_m^n = 50$ s. The horizontal lines quantize $v_k(t)$ into $X = 4$ values that form the finite set $\mathcal{X} = \{-30, 0, 30, 60\}$. The purple star and the blue square denote the values of $\bar{v}_k \cdot T^{pl}$ and $\bar{v}_k^{qu} \cdot T^{pl}$, respectively, at each generation stage $k \in \mathcal{K}_m^n$

Definition 5.1 Let $\bar{v}_k \in \mathbb{R}$ and $\bar{v}_k^{qu} \in X$ denote the user's Average Attention Level (AAL) and Quantized Average Attention Level (QAAL) over generation stage $k \in \mathcal{K}_m^n$, respectively. They are measured by the improvement in CAL and the quantized value of the CAL improvement per unit time, i.e., $\bar{v}_k := v_k(T^{pl})/T^{pl}$ and $\bar{v}_k^{qu} := v_k^{qu}(T^{pl})/T^{pl}$, respectively.

5.2.4   Q-Learning via Consolidated Data

In Sect. 5.2.4, we elaborate on the adaptive learning block (i.e., Step 5 in Fig. 5.1). Since the inspection time of a user reading one email is not sufficiently long, we consolidate a group of email inspection data to learn the optimal visual-aid generation policy over a population.

The QAAL $\bar{v}_k^{qu} \in X$ represents the attention state at the generation stage $k \in \mathcal{K}_m^n$. Since the goal is to enhance the user's attention represented by the CAL, the reward function $R : X \times \mathcal{A} \mapsto \mathbb{R}$ should be monotone concerning the value of $\bar{v}_k^{qu}$, e.g., $R(\bar{v}_k^{qu}, a_k) := \bar{v}_k^{qu}, \forall a_k \in \mathcal{A}$. In this work, we assume that each visual aid $a_k \in \mathcal{A}$ exerts the same statistical effect on the attention process regardless of different users and emails. Thus, we can consolidate the data set of $\bar{M} \in \{1, \cdots, M\}$ users and $\bar{N} \in \{1, \cdots, N\}$ emails[2] to learn the optimal visual-aid generation policy $\sigma \in \Sigma : X \mapsto \mathcal{A}$ in a total of $\bar{K} := \sum_{m=1}^{\bar{M}} \sum_{n=1}^{\bar{N}} K_m^n$ stages. With a given discounted factor $\beta \in (0, 1)$, the expected long-term objective can be represented as $\max_{\sigma \in \Sigma} \mathbb{E}[\sum_{k=1}^{\bar{K}} (\beta)^k \cdot R(\bar{v}_k^{qu}, \sigma(\bar{v}_k^{qu}))]$.

The Q-table $[Q_k(\bar{v}_k^{qu}, a_k)]_{\bar{v}_k^{qu} \in X, a_k \in \mathcal{A}}$ represents the user's attention pattern at generation stage $k \in \bar{\mathcal{K}} := \{1, \cdots, \bar{K}\}$, i.e., the estimated payoff of applying visual aid $a_k \in \mathcal{A}$ when the attention state is $\bar{v}_k^{qu} \in X$. Let the sequence of learning rate $\gamma_k(\bar{v}_k^{qu}, a_k)$ satisfy the convergence condition in Chap. 2. Then, we can update the attention pattern at each generation stage $k \in \bar{\mathcal{K}}$ as follows, i.e.,

$$
\begin{aligned}
Q_{k+1}(\bar{v}_k^{qu}, \sigma_k(\bar{v}_k^{qu})) &= Q_k(\bar{v}_k^{qu}, \sigma_k(\bar{v}_k^{qu})) \\
&\quad + \gamma_k(\bar{v}_k^{qu}, \sigma_k(\bar{v}_k^{qu})) \cdot [R(\bar{v}_k^{qu}, \sigma_k(\bar{v}_k^{qu})) \\
&\quad + \beta \max_{a \in \mathcal{A}} Q_k(\bar{v}_{k+1}^{qu}, a) - Q_k(\bar{v}_k^{qu}, \sigma_k(\bar{v}_k^{qu}))],
\end{aligned}
\tag{5.2}
$$

where the visual-aid generation policy $\sigma_k(\bar{v}_k^{qu})$ at generation stage $k \in \bar{\mathcal{K}}$ is an ϵ_k-greedy policy defined in Chap. 2.

---

[2] When sufficiently large data sets are available, we can carefully choose these $\bar{M}$ users to share similar attributes (e.g., ages, sexes, races, etc.) and these $\bar{N}$ emails to belongs to the same categories (e.g., business or personal emails).

5.3   Phishing Prevention Mechanism

The attention enhancement mechanism in Sect. 5.2 tracks the attention process in real-time to enable the adaptive visual-aid generation. By properly modifying the user's attention and engaging him in vetting emails, the attention enhancement mechanism serves as a stepping-stone to achieving the ultimate goal of phishing prevention. Empirical evidence and observations have shown that a high attention level, or mental arousal, does not necessarily yield good performance [7]. In the specific task of phishing recognition, recent works [1, 6] have also identified curvilinear relationships between phishing recognition accuracy and critical attention factors, including a participant's cue utilization, cognitive reflection, and cognitive load. Thus, besides attention metrics, e.g., the AAL, we need to design anti-phishing metrics to measure the users' performance of phishing recognition as will be shown in Sect. 5.3.1.

In Sect. 5.3.2, we develop an efficient meta-level algorithm to tune the hyperparameters (e.g., the period length T^{pl} of the visual-aid generation, the number of attention states X, the attention scores $r^{co}(s), \alpha(s), \forall s \in \mathcal{S}$, etc.) in the attention enhancement mechanism. We denote these hyperparameters as one d-dimensional variable $\theta = [T^{pl}, X, [r^{co}(s)]_{s \in \mathcal{S}}, [\alpha(s)]_{s \in \mathcal{S}}] \in \mathbb{R}^d$, where $d = 2 + 2|\mathcal{S}|$. Let the i-th element θ^i be upper and lower bounded by $\bar{\theta}^i$ and $\underline{\theta}^i$, respectively. Thus, $\theta \in \Theta^d := \{[\theta^i]_{i \in \{1, \cdots, d\}} \subset \mathbb{R}^d | \underline{\theta}^i < \theta^i < \bar{\theta}^i\}$.

5.3.1   Metrics for Phishing Recognition

As illustrated by Step 7 in Fig. 5.1, we provide a metric to evaluate the outcome of the users' phishing identification under a given hyperparameter $\theta \in \Theta^d$. After vetting email $n \in \{1, \cdots, \bar{N}\}$, the user $m \in \{1, \cdots, \bar{M}\}$ judges the email to be phishing or legitimate. The binary variable $z_m^n(\theta) \in \{z^{co}, z^{wr}\}$ represents whether the judgment is correct (denoted by z^{co}) or not (denoted by z^{wr}). We can reshape the two-dimension index (m, n) as a one-dimension index $\hat{n}$ and rewrite $z_m^n(\theta)$ as $z_{\hat{n}}(\theta)$. Once these users have judged in total of N^{bo} emails, we define the following metric $c^{ac} \in C : \Theta^d \mapsto [0, 1]$ to evaluate the *accuracy* of phishing recognition, i.e.,

$$c^{ac}(\theta) := \frac{1}{N^{bo}} \sum_{\hat{n}=1}^{N^{bo}} |\mathbf{1}_{\{z_{\hat{n}}(\theta)=z^{co}\}}|, \forall \theta \in \Theta^d. \tag{5.3}$$

The goal is to find the optimal hyperparameter $\theta^* \in \Theta^d$ to maximize the accuracy of phishing identification, i.e., $\theta^* \in \arg\max_{\theta \in \Theta^d} c^{ac}(\theta)$. However, we cannot know the value of $c^{ac}(\theta)$ for a $\theta \in \Theta^d$ a priori until we implement this hyperparameter θ in the attention enhancement mechanism. The implemented hyperparameter affects the adaptive visual-aid generation that changes the user's attention and the anti-phishing performance metric $c^{ac}(\theta)$. Since the experimental evaluation at a given $\theta \in \Theta^d$ is time-consuming, we present an algorithm in Sect. 5.3.2 to determine how to choose and update the hyperparameter to maximize the detection accuracy.

5.3.2 Efficient Hyperparameter Tuning

We illustrate the meta-adaptation (i.e., Step 8 in Fig. 5.1) in Sect. 5.3.2. As illustrated in Fig. 5.6, we refer to the duration of every N^{bo} security decision as a *tuning stage*. Consider a time and budget limit that restricts us to conduct L tuning stages in total. We denote θ_l as the hyperparameter at the l-th tuning stage where $l \in \mathcal{L} := \{1, 2, \cdots, L\}$. Since each user's email inspection time is different, each tuning stage can contain different numbers of generation stages.

To find the optimal hyperparameter $\theta^* \in \Theta^d$ within L tuning stages is challenging. The empirical methods (e.g., a naive grid search or a random search over $\Theta^d \subset \mathbb{R}^d$) become inefficient when $d > 1$. BO [4] provides a systematic way to update the hyperparameter and balance between exploration and exploitation. BO consists of a Bayesian statistical model of the objective function $c^{ac} \in C$ and an acquisition function for deciding the hyperparameter to implement at the next tuning stage. The statistical model of $c^{ac} \in C$ is a Gaussian process $\mathcal{N}(\mu^0, \Sigma^0)$ with a mean function $\mu^0(\theta) = \bar{\mu}^0$ and covariance function or kernel $\Sigma^0(\theta, \bar{\theta}) = \lambda^0 \cdot \exp(\sum_{i=1}^{d} \lambda^i (\theta^i - \bar{\theta}^i)^2)$ for all $\theta, \bar{\theta} \in \Theta^d$, where $\bar{\mu}^0$, λ^0 and $\lambda^i, i \in \{1, 2, \cdots, d\}$, are parameters of the kernel. The kernel Σ^0 is required to be positive semi-definite and has the property that the points closer in the input space are more strongly correlated. For any $l \in \mathcal{L}$, we define three shorthand notations

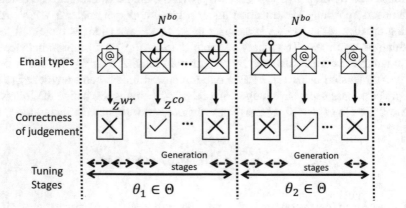

Fig. 5.6 Hyperparameter tuning based on the user's phishing recognition. Each tuning stage consists of N^{bo} emails and contains several generation stages

$\mu^0(\theta_{1:l}) := [\mu^0(\theta_1), \cdots, \mu^0(\theta_l)]$, $c^{ac}(\theta_{1:l}) := [c^{ac}(\theta_1), \cdots, c^{ac}(\theta_l)]$, and

$$\Sigma^0(\theta_{1:l}, \theta_{1:l}) := \begin{bmatrix} \Sigma^0(\theta_1, \theta_1) & \cdots & \Sigma^0(\theta_1, \theta_l) \\ \vdots & \ddots & \vdots \\ \Sigma^0(\theta_l, \theta_1) & \cdots & \Sigma^0(\theta_l, \theta_l) \end{bmatrix}.$$

Then, the evaluation vector of $l \in \mathcal{L}$ elements is assumed to be multivariate Gaussian distributed, i.e., $c^{ac}(\theta_{1:l}) \sim \mathcal{N}(\mu^0(\theta_{1:l}), \Sigma^0(\theta_{1:l}, \theta_{1:l}))$. Conditioned on the values of $\theta_{1:l}$, we can infer the value of $c^{ac}(\theta)$ at any other $\theta \in \Theta \setminus \{\theta_{l'}\}_{l' \in \{1, \cdots, l\}}$ by Bayesian rule, i.e.,

$$c^{ac}(\theta) | c^{ac}(\theta_{1:l}) \sim \mathcal{N}(\mu^n(\theta), (\Sigma^n(\theta))^2), \tag{5.4}$$

where $\mu^n(\theta) = \Sigma^0(\theta, \theta_{1:l}) \cdot \Sigma^0(\theta_{1:l}, \theta_{1:l})^{-1} \cdot (c^{ac}(\theta_{1:l}) - \mu^0(\theta_{1:l})) + \mu^0(\theta)$ and $(\Sigma^n(\theta))^2 = \Sigma^0(\theta, \theta) - \Sigma^0(\theta, \theta_{1:l}) \cdot \Sigma^0(\theta, \theta_{1:l})^{-1} \cdot \Sigma^0(\theta_{1:l}, \theta)$.

We adopt *expected improvement* as the acquisition function. Define $c_l^* := \max_{l' \in \{1, \cdots, l\}} c^{ac}(\theta_{l'})$ as the optimal evaluation among the first l evaluations and a shorthand notation $(c^{ac}(\theta) - c_l^*)^+ := \max\{c^{ac}(\theta) - c_l^*, 0\}$. For any $l \in \mathcal{L}$, we define $\mathbb{E}_l[\cdot] := \mathbb{E}[\cdot | c^{ac}(\theta_{1:l})]$ as the expectation taken under the posterior distribution of $c^{ac}(\theta)$ conditioned on the values of l evaluations $c^{ac}(\theta_{1:l})$. Then, the expected improvement is $\text{EI}_l(\theta) := \mathbb{E}_l[(c^{ac}(\theta) - c_l^*)^+]$. The hyperparameter at the next tuning stage is chosen to maximize the expected improvement at the current stage, i.e,

$$\theta_{l+1} \in \arg\max_{\theta \in \Theta^d} \text{EI}_l(\theta). \tag{5.5}$$

The expected improvement can be evaluated in a closed form, and (5.5) can be computed inexpensively by gradient methods [4].

At the first $L^0 \in \{1, 2, \cdots, L\}$ tuning stages, we choose the hyperparameter $\theta_l, l \in \{1, 2, \cdots, L^0\}$, uniformly from Θ^d. We can use the evaluation results $c^{ac}(\theta_l), l \in \{1, 2, \cdots, L^0\}$, to determine the parameters $\bar{\mu}^0, \lambda^0$, and $\lambda^i, i \in \{1, 2, \cdots, d\}$, by Maximum Likelihood Estimation (MLE); i.e., we determine the values of these parameters so that they maximize the likelihood of observing the vector $[c^{ac}(\theta_{1:L^0})]$. For the remaining $L - L^0$ tuning stages, we choose $\theta_l, l \in \{L^0, L^0 + 1, \cdots, L\}$, in sequence as summarized in Algorithm 1.

5.4 Case Study

In this case study, we verify the effectiveness of ADVERT via a data set collected from human subject experiments conducted at New York University [2].

The data set involves $M = 160$ undergraduate students ($n_{\text{White}} = 27$, $n_{\text{Black}} = 19$, $n_{\text{Asian}} = 64$, $n_{\text{Hispanic/Latinx}} = 17$, $n_{\text{other}} = 33$) who are asked to vet $N = 12$

Algorithm 1: Hyperparameter tuning via BO

---

1 Implement the initial L^0 evaluations $c^{ac}(\theta_l), l \in \{1, 2, \cdots, L^0\}$;

2 Place a Gaussian process prior on $c^{ac} \in C$, i.e., $c^{ac}(\theta_{1:L^0}) \sim \mathcal{N}(\mu^0(\theta_{1:L^0}), \Sigma^0(\theta_{1:L^0}, \theta_{1:L^0}))$;

3 for $l \leftarrow L^0$ **to** L **do**

4 | **Obtain** the posterior distribution of $c^{ac}(\theta)$ in (5.4) based on the existing l evaluations;

5 | **Compute** $\mathrm{EI}_l(\theta), \forall \theta \in \Theta^d$, based on the posterior distribution;

6 | **Determine** θ_{l+1} via (5.5);

7 | **Implement** θ_{l+1} at the next tuning stage $l + 1$ to evaluate $c^{ac}(\theta_{l+1})$;

8 end

9 Return the maximized value of all observed samples, i.e., $\theta^* \in \arg\max_{\theta_l \in \{\theta_1, \cdots, \theta_L\}} c^{ac}(\theta_l)$;

---

different emails (e.g., the email of NYU friends network in Fig. 5.2) separately and then give a rating of how likely they would take actions solicited in the emails (e.g., maintain membership in Fig. 5.2). When presented to different participants, each email is described as either posing a cyber threat or risk-free legitimate opportunities to investigate how the above description affects the participants' phishing recognition.

While the participants vet the emails, the Tobii Pro T60XL eye-tracking monitor records their eye locations on a 1920×1200 resolution screen and the current pupil diameters of both eyes with a sampling rate of 60 Hz. Figure 5.7 illustrates the time-expanded eye-gaze trajectory of a participant vetting the sample email in Fig. 5.2. The z-coordinate of a 3D point (x, y, z) represents the time when the participant gazes at the pixel (x, y) in the email area. The participant's eye gaze locations move progressively from the points in warmer color to the ones in cooler color. Figure 5.7 illustrates the zigzag pattern of the participant's eye-gaze trajectory; i.e., the participant reads emails from left to right and top to bottom. The participant starts with the title, spends the majority of time on the main content, and glances at other AoIs (e.g., the links and the signatures). There is also a small chance of revisiting the email content and looking outside the email area.

Figure 5.8 illustrates the participant's pupil sizes of left and right eyes in red and blue, respectively, concerning the same trial of the data set to generate Fig. 5.7. At different times, the average of the pupil diameters (resp. gaze locations) of the right and left eyes represent the pupil size (resp. gaze location). Following Sect. 5.2.1, we obtain the 15 VSs illustrated by the grey squares in Fig. 5.8 based on the gaze locations of the email pixels in Fig. 5.7. Since the covert eye-tracking system does not require head-mounted equipment or chinrests, the tracking can occur without the participants' awareness. We refer the reader to the supplement materials of [2] for the survey data and the details of the experimental procedure.[3]

---

[3] The processed data used in this manuscript, including the temporal transitions of AoIs and the pupil sizes, is available at https://osf.io/4y32d/.

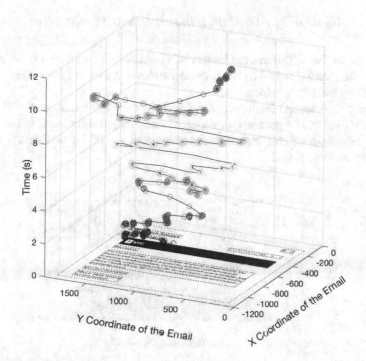

Fig. 5.7 A time-expanded plot of a typical eye-gaze trajectory with a sampling rate of 60 Hz. The *x*-*y* plane (in the unit of pixels) represents the email area. The *z*-axis represents the time (in the unit of seconds) of the participant's eye-gaze trajectory. The warmer color indicates a smaller value on the *z*-axis (i.e., an earlier gaze of the point)

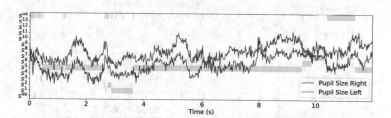

Fig. 5.8 Gaze locations and pupil sizes collected in the trial of the data set illustrated in Fig. 5.7. The grey squares illustrate the transition of 15 VSs. The red and blue lines represent the variations of the participant's left and right pupil sizes, respectively, as he reads the email. The *x*-axis represents the time (in the unit of seconds) during the email inspection

5.4.1   Validation of Attention Enhancement Mechanism

Figure 5.9 further illustrates the impact of visual aids a^N and a^Y on the AAL in red and blue, respectively. The figure demonstrates that a^Y can increase the mean of AAL yet increase its variance.

We plot the entire Q-learning updates with $N^{bo} = 100$ emails in Fig. 5.10 that contains a total of 609 generations stages. The learning results show that the visual aid a^Y outweighs a^N for both attention states and should be persistently applied under the current setting.

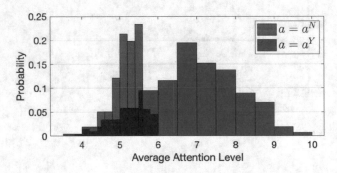

Fig. 5.9 The normalized histogram of average attention level under visual aids a^N and a^Y in red and blue, respectively

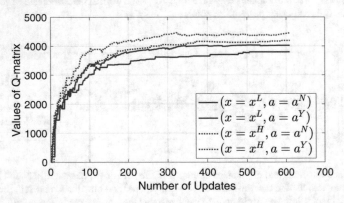

Fig. 5.10 The Q-learning updates under hyperparameters $X^{at} = 5.56$ and $T^{pl} = 3$ s. The red and blue lines represent the Q-matrix values under visual aids a^N and a^Y, respectively. The solid and dashed lines represent the Q-matrix values under attention states x^L and x^H, respectively

5.4.2 Validation of Phishing Prevention Mechanism

As explained in Sect. 5.3, for each different application scenario, a meta optimization of the accuracy metric $c^{ac}(X^{at}, T^{pl})$ is required to find the optimal attention threshold X^{at} and the period length T^{pl} for visual-aid generation. To obtain the value of $c^{ac}(X^{at}, T^{pl})$ under different values of the hyperparameter $\theta = [X^{at}, T^{pl}]$, we need to implement the hyperparameter and repeat for n^{rp} times to reduce the noise. Thus, the evaluation is costly, and Bayesian Optimization (BO) in Algorithm 1 is a favorable method to achieve the meta optimization. We illustrate the Bayesian Optimization (BO) for $L = 60$ tuning stages in Fig. 5.11. Each blue point represents the average value of $c^{ac}(X^{at}, T^{pl})$ over $n^{rp} = 20$ repeated samples under the hyperparameter $\theta = [X^{at}, T^{pl}]$. Based on the estimated Gaussian model in red, we observe that the attention threshold $X^{at} \in [1, 33]$ has a small impact on phishing recognition while the period length $T^{pl} \in [60, 600]$ has a periodic impact on phishing recognition. The optimal hyperparameters for phishing prevention are $X^{at,*} = 8.8347$ and $T^{pl,*} = 6.63$ s.

We illustrate the temporal procedure of Bayesian Optimization (BO) for $L = 60$ tuning stages in Fig. 5.12. As we increase the number of tuning stages to obtain more samples, the maximized value of the accuracy metric $c^{ac} \in C$ monotonously increases as shown in red. The blue line and its error bar represent the mean and variances of the sample values at each tuning stage, respectively. Throughout the

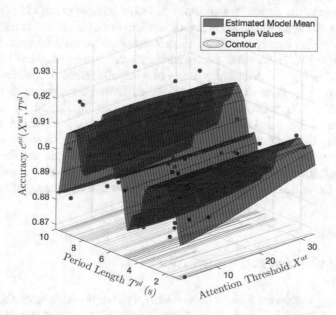

Fig. 5.11 The estimated Gaussian model of the objective function $c^{ac}(\theta)$ concerning the hyperparameter $\theta = [X^{at}, T^{pl}]$ in red with its contour on the bottom. The blue points represent the sample values of 60 tuning stages

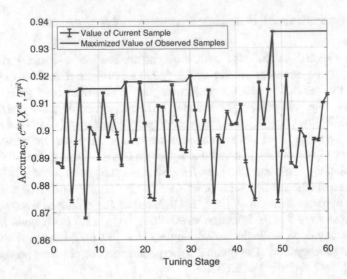

Fig. 5.12 Accuracy metric $c^{ac}(X^{at}, T^{pl})$ at $L = 60$ tuning stages. The blue line and its error bar represent the mean value of the samples and their variances, respectively. The red line represents the maximized value of the observed samples up to the current tuning stage

$L = 60$ tuning stages, the variance remains small, which indicates that ADVERT is *robust* to the noise of human attention and decision processes.

Compared to the benchmark accuracy of 74.6% without visual aids, participants with visual aid achieve the accuracy of a minimum of 86% under all 60 tuning stages of different hyperparameters. The above accuracy improvement corroborates that the ADVERT's attention enhancement mechanism highlighted by the blue background in Fig. 5.1 effectively serves as a stepping stone to facilitate phishing recognition. The results shown in the blue line further corroborate the efficiency of the ADVERT's phishing prevention mechanism highlighted by the orange background in Fig. 5.1; i.e., in less than 50 tuning stages, we manage to improve the accuracy of phishing recognition from 86.8% to 93.7%. Besides, the largest accuracy improvement (from 88.7% to 91.4%) happens within the first 3 tuning stages. Thus, if we have to reduce the number of tuning stages due to budget limits, ADVERT can still achieve a sufficient improvement in the accuracy of recognizing phishing.

5.5   Conclusions and Future Work

As a prototypical *innate human vulnerability*, lack of attention is one of the main challenges to protecting users from phishing attacks. To address the challenge, we have developed a *human-technical solution* called ADVERT to guide the users' attention to the right contents of the email and consequently improve their accuracy of phishing recognition.

The future work would focus on designing a more sophisticated visual support system that can determine when and how to generate visual aids in lieu of a periodic generation. We may also embed ADVERT into VR/AR technologies to mitigate human vulnerabilities under simulated deception scenarios, where the simulated environment can be easily repeated or changed. Finally, there would be an opportunity to incorporate factors such as pressure and incentives into the design by limiting the participant's vetting time and providing rewards for accurately identifying phishing, respectively.

References

1. Ackerley M, Morrison B, Ingrey K, Wiggins M, Bayl-Smith P, Morrison N (2022) Errors, irregularities, and misdirection: cue utilisation and cognitive reflection in the diagnosis of phishing emails. Australas J Inf Syst 26:1–21. https://doi.org/10.3127/ajis.v26i0.3615
2. Cox EB, Zhu Q, Balcetis E (2020) Stuck on a phishing lure: differential use of base rates in self and social judgments of susceptibility to cyber risk. Compr Results Soc Psychol 4(1):25–52
3. Dhamija R, Tygar JD, Hearst M (2006) Why phishing works. In: Proc. of the SIGCHI conference on human factors in computing systems, pp 581–590
4. Frazier PI (2018) Bayesian optimization. In: Recent advances in optimization and modeling of contemporary problems, INFORMS, pp 255–278
5. Huang L, Jia S, Balcetis E, Zhu Q (2022) Advert: an adaptive and data-driven attention enhancement mechanism for phishing prevention. IEEE Trans Inf Forens Secur 17:2585–2597
6. Nasser G, Morrison BW, Bayl-Smith P, Taib R, Gayed M, Wiggins MW (2020) The role of cue utilization and cognitive load in the recognition of phishing emails. Front Big Data 3:1–10. https://doi.org/10.3389/fdata.2020.546860
7. Posner MI, Marin OS (2016) Attention and performance XI. Routledge

Chapter 6
RADAMS: Defending Against Proactive Attention Attacks

Abstract Following the definition in Sect. 1.2.3.2, in this chapter, we identify and formally define a new type of proactive attention attacks called Informational Denial-of-Service (IDoS) attacks that generate a large volume of feint attacks to overload human operators and hide real attacks among feints. We incorporate human factors (e.g., levels of expertise, stress, and efficiency) and empirical psychological results (e.g., the Yerkes–Dodson law and the sunk cost fallacy) to model the operators' attention dynamics and their decision-making processes along with the real-time alert monitoring and inspection. To assist human operators in dismissing the feints and escalating the real attacks timely and accurately, we develop a Resilient and Adaptive Data-driven alert and Attention Management Strategy (RADAMS) that de-emphasizes alerts selectively based on the abstracted category labels of the alerts. RADAMS uses Reinforcement Learning (RL) to achieve a customized and transferable design for various human operators and evolving IDoS attacks. The integrated modeling and theoretical analysis lead to the Product Principle of Attention (PPoA), fundamental limits, and the tradeoff among crucial human and economic factors.

Keywords Proactive attention vulnerability · Feint attacks · Reinforcement learning · Risk analysis · Cognitive load · Alert fatigue

6.1 Introduction

Figure 6.1 illustrates the analogy between Denial-of-Service (DoS) attacks in CPS and Informational Denial-of-Service (IDoS) attacks in HCPSs. Following Sect. 1.2.5.2, DoS and IDoS attacks compromise the availability of information security and cognitive security by depleting the limited computing resources and cognitive resources, respectively. In particular, DoS attacks generate a large number of superfluous requests to prevent the targeted machines from fulfilling service requests, while IDoS attacks create a large amount of unrelated information to prevent human operators from acquiring the knowledge contained in the unprocessed information.

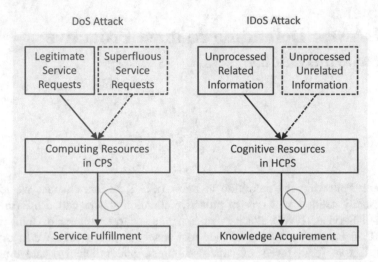

Fig. 6.1 An analogy of DoS and IDoS attacks that compromise the availability of information security and cognitive security, in green and blue, respectively. The processing processes with and without attacks are illustrated in dashed and solid lines, respectively

DoS attacks can target network layer (e.g., ICMP/IMGP flood, Teardrop attack, and Smurf attack), transmission layer (e.g., SYN/SYN-ACK/UDP/RST/DNS flood), and application layer (e.g., HTTP/SIP flood, DNS/SNMP/NTP amplification attack). Analogously, IDoS attacks can target multiple assailable cognitive resources, including attention, memory and learning capacity, and reasoning. Among all these assailable cognitive resources, we focus on attention to illustrate the impact and defense of IDoS attacks in the following subsections. We provide the following alert response scenario in a control room as a prototypical example of attentional IDoS attacks, where the timeline is illustrated in Fig. 6.2. The real and feint alerts in the example are unprocessed related and unrelated information, respectively, in Fig. 6.1.

Example 6.1.1 (IDoS Attack Timeline in a Control Room) It is 11 p.m. in the night. The IDoS attacker successfully gains access to a set of controllers and sensors in a nuclear power plant and plans to gradually deviate the temperature to reduce production rate and cause damage to the core reactor. However, before he launches the attack on the temperature controller, he intentionally triggers excessive alerts of abnormal pressure in another reactor. He can trigger these feint alerts either by compromising the reading of the pressure sensors or by actually changing the pressure in that reactor.

At 11:10 p.m., an operator of a nuclear control room begins to receive excessive alerts of abnormal pressure, as illustrated in Fig. 6.3. On the one hand, the exploration of alerts, the urgency, and the high risk of nuclear plants greatly increase the cognitive load of the human operator, causing high pressure and negative

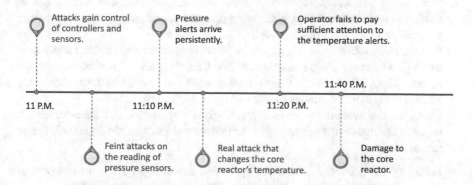

Fig. 6.2 Timeline of the attentional IDoS attack in a nuclear control room. The events related to attacks and the resulting outcomes are illustrated in red and black, respectively

Fig. 6.3 An operator's view of alert response in a control room. Prioritized and classified messages and alerts are generated from sensors and controllers at different locations

emotions. On the other hand, the persistent arrival of new alerts keeps interrupting the human operator's cognitive process, thereby delaying the knowledge acquisition in Fig. 6.1, i.e., figuring out the causes, impacts, and mitigation methods. The above two reasons lead to the regrettable outcome; i.e., the operator fails to pay sufficient and sustained attention to the alerts of the temperature controller that arrive at 11:20 p.m., which leads to the damage of the core reactor in 20 min.

The example illustrates the following three security challenges of attentional IDoS attacks.

- First, IDoS attacks exploit the existing alert fatigue problem in the age of infobesity and intensify it by generating feint alerts and intentionally increasing the percentage of false-positive alerts.
- Second, IDoS attacks directly target the human operators and security analysts in the SOC who are in charge of defending the CPS and play the role of the immune system. Thus, IDoS attacks can be analogous to the Human Immunodeficiency Virus (HIV), which damages the human immune system.
- Third, as the system becomes increasingly complicated and time-critical, it requires operators of high expertise to understand the domain information and identify feints.

Following the defense methods in Fig. 1.8, we can mitigate IDoS attacks by user training and mechanism design, cyber defense, and the AI-powered enhancer.

- The first method provides social solutions. On the one hand, by training human operators to deal with the cognitive overload, they become more experienced at remaining vigilant and productive under a heavy cognitive load. On the other hand, the total cognitive load to accomplish the task can be shared by recruiting more human operators.
- The second method is technical and includes three components of threat detection, alert filtering, and alert triage, as shown in the dashed black box of Fig. 6.4. Threat detection generates alerts that contain *device-level* contextual information, including the software version, hardware parameters, existing vulnerabilities, and security patches. Alert filtering and triage techniques automatically select and prioritize alerts based on established techniques (e.g., [1, 4, 7]) and the *system-level* properties of the alerts (e.g., time sensitivity, susceptibility, complexity, and criticality) that are abstracted from *device-level* contextual information.
- The third method, illustrated by the dashed blue box of Fig. 6.4, is social-technical. It incorporates both the knowledge of human attention and RL techniques to pinpoint critical alerts for human operators, filter the information to be processed, and alleviate their cognitive loads.

For the first method, attention training can be time-consuming, and its effectiveness is not guaranteed. Cognitive load sharing requires the coordination of the operator team and can incur additional costs in human resources. The second method has been applied and has greatly reduced the number of alerts to be processed. However, as alerts increase with the wide application of Internet of Things (IoT) sensors and the incoming feint attacks, the demand for real-time alert investigation still far outweighs the supply of human operators' attention resources. Thus, we required the third method of attention-aware alert selection to manage human attention limitations and proactively prevent cognitive overload.

The first method aims to increase the capacity of the cognitive resources in Fig. 6.1. The second and third methods preprocess the unprocessed information at *technical* and *cognitive* levels, respectively, so that it adapts to the capacity and characteristics of the existing cognitive resources.

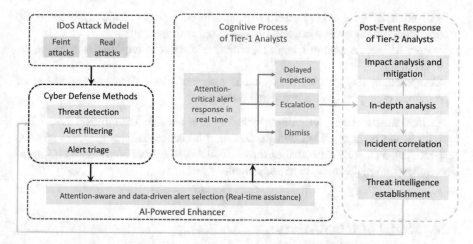

Fig. 6.4 The overview diagram of IDoS attacks, cyber defense methods, the AI-powered enhancer, the real-time manual alert inspection process, and the post-event analysis in red, black, blue, green, and gray boxes, respectively. Following the hierarchical alert analysis in SOC [8], tier-1 SOC analysts, or the operators, are in charge of monitoring, inspecting, and responding to alerts in real time. After tier-1 analysts escalate alerts, tier-2 SOC analysts analyze them in-depth that can last hours to months. The post-event analysis can establish threat intelligence that are incorporated to improve the cyber defense methods

Figure 6.4 illustrates the overview diagram of the system models. After presenting the motivation and features of feints in Sect. 6.2, we illustrate the models of IDoS attacks, cyber defense, human attention process of alert investigation, and AI-powered enhancer in Sects. 6.3, 6.4, 6.5, and 6.6, respectively.

6.2   Motivation and Features of Feints

Feint is a widely-used concept in sports and military tactics that refers to maneuvers designed to distract or mislead. There are many real-life examples (e.g., the Normandy landing) where feint attacks or feint retreats are used to win wars. We have also witnessed feints in the following biodeception example [6], where hepatitis B combats the immune system by overwhelming the immune system with decoy particles that bind antibodies.[1] Although these particles do not cause disease, they deplete the limited antibodies that could bind to the virus and stop the infection. In this work, we make an analogy of the feints in cyberspace to the ones in sports, the military, and biology. We identify the following features for cyber feints.

---

[1] Available at https://www.youtube.com/watch?v=Iq5nFg-H0xo.

- The goals of feint attacks are to trigger a large volume of alerts, increase the operators' cognitive burden, and distract them from real attacks.
- With a deliberate goal of triggering alerts, feint attacks require fewer resources to craft.
- Compared to real attacks, feint attacks may not cause devastating damage or require a prompt response to prevent damage.

In the real-life attack incidents, including the ones in Examples 1.2.1, 1.2.2, and 1.2.3, we refer to DDoS attacks and data breaches as feint and real attacks, respectively, as the ultimate goal of these attacks is to extract confidential information rather than make the system unavailable.

6.3   Model of IDoS Attacks

We model IDoS attack as a sequence of feint and real attacks of heterogeneous targets, which can be characterized by the 4-tuple $(\Theta, \Phi, \mathcal{K}_{AT}, \mathcal{Z})$. The red arrows in Fig. 6.5 illustrate the sequential arrival of feints and real attacks.

- $\Theta := \{\theta_{FE}, \theta_{RE}\}$ is the set of attacks' types, where θ_{FE} and θ_{RE} represent feint and real attacks, respectively.
- Φ is the set of the potential attack targets, including cyber assets (e.g., servers, databases, and workstations) and physical assets (e.g., sensors of pressure, temperature, and flow rate).
- We model the stochastic arrival of feints and real attacks as a Markov renewal process where $t^k, k \in \mathbb{Z}^{0+}$, is the time of the k-th arrival.[2]

  - $\kappa_{AT} \in \mathcal{K}_{AT} : \Theta \times \Phi \times \Theta \times \Phi \mapsto [0, 1]$ is the transition kernel, where $\kappa_{AT}(\theta^{k+1}, \phi^{k+1}|\theta^k, \phi^k)$ denotes the probability that the $(k + 1)$-th attack has type $\theta^{k+1} \in \Theta$ and target $\phi^{k+1} \in \Phi$ when the k-th attack has type $\theta^k \in \Theta$ and target $\phi^k \in \Phi$.
  - The inter-arrival time $\tau^k := t^{k+1} - t^k$ is a continuous random variable with support $[0, \infty)$ and Probability Density Function (PDF) $z \in \mathcal{Z} : \Theta \times \Phi \times \Theta \times \Phi \mapsto \mathbb{R}^{0+}$, where $z(t|\theta^{k+1}, \phi^{k+1}, \theta^k, \phi^k)$ is the probability that the inter-arrival time is t when the attacks' types and targets at attack stage k and $k + 1$ are θ^k, ϕ^k and θ^{k+1}, ϕ^{k+1}, respectively.

---

[2] We refer to the k-th attack equivalently as the attack at *attack stage* $k \in \mathbb{Z}^{0+}$ and let $\theta^k \in \Theta$ and $\phi^k \in \Phi$ be the attack's type and target at attack stage $k \in \mathbb{Z}^{0+}$, respectively.

6.4   Model of Alert Triage

Following Sect. 6.3, human operators cannot directly know the the type θ^k and target ϕ^k of the attack at attack stage $k \in \mathbb{Z}^{0+}$. Equipped with the cyber defense methods denoted by the black box in Fig. 6.4, we assume that these sequentially arriving attacks can trigger alerts with zero delay, as illustrated by the blue arrows in Fig. 6.5.

These alerts contain observable *device-level* contextual information, including the software version, hardware parameters, existing vulnerabilities, and security patches. The contextual information contains valuable details for in-depth analysis, but it usually cannot be processed in real time by AI-powered enhancer in Sect. 6.6 or tier-1 operators in Sect. 6.5. Thus, cyber defense methods can incorporate an alert triage process to map the device-level information to *system-level* metrics that helps human operators make timely responses. Some essential metrics are listed as follows.

- **Source** $s_{SO} \in \mathcal{S}_{SO}$: The sensors of an industrial control system or the cyber assets that the alerts are associated with.
- **Time Sensitivity** $s_{TS} \in \mathcal{S}_{TS}$: The length of time that the potential attack needs to achieve its attack goals.
- **Complexity** $s_{CO} \in \mathcal{S}_{CO}$: The degree of effort that a human operator takes to inspect the alert.
- **Susceptibility** $s_{SU} \in \mathcal{S}_{SU}$: The likelihood that the attack succeeds and inflicts damage on the protected system.
- **Criticality** $s_{CR} \in \mathcal{S}_{CR}$: The consequence or the impact of the attack's damage.

These *observable* alert metrics form the *category label* of an alert. We define the category label associated with the k-th alert as $s^k := (s^k_{SO}, s^k_{TS}, s^k_{CO}, s^k_{SU}, s^k_{CR}) \in \mathcal{S}$, where $\mathcal{S} := \mathcal{S}_{SO} \times \mathcal{S}_{TS} \times \mathcal{S}_{CO} \times \mathcal{S}_{SU} \times \mathcal{S}_{CR}$. The joint set $\mathcal{S}$ can be adapted to suit the organization's needs in the security practice. For example, we have $\mathcal{S}_{TS} = \emptyset$ if time sensitivity is unavailable or unimportant.

The technical-level alert triage process establishes a stochastic connection between the hidden types and targets of the IDoS attacks and the observable

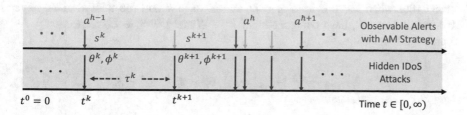

Fig. 6.5 The timeline of an IDoS attack and alerts under Attention Management (AM) strategies in orange and blue, respectively. The red arrows represent the sequential arrival of feints and real attacks. The non-transparent and semi-transparent blue arrows indicate the emphasized and de-emphasized alerts, respectively

category labels of the associated alerts. Let $o(s^k|\theta^k, \phi^k)$ be the probability of obtaining category label $s^k \in \mathcal{S}$, when the associated attack has type $\theta^k \in \Theta$ and target $\phi^k \in \Phi$. The revelation kernel o reflects the quality of the alert triage. For example, feints with lightweight resource consumption usually have a limited impact. Thus, a high-quality triage process should classify the associated alert as low criticality with a high probability. Letting $b(\theta^k, \phi^k)$ denote the probability that the k-th attack has type θ^k and target ϕ^k at the steady-state, we can compute the steady-state distribution b in closed form based on κ_{AT}. Then, the transition of category labels at different attack stages is also Markov and is represented by $\kappa_{CL} \in \mathcal{K}_{CL} : \mathcal{S} \times \mathcal{S} \mapsto [0, 1]$. We can compute $\kappa_{CL} = \frac{\Pr(s^{k+1}, s^k)}{\sum_{s^{k+1} \in \mathcal{S}} \Pr(s^{k+1}, s^k)}$ based on κ_{AT}, o, b, where $\Pr(s^{k+1}, s^k) = \sum_{\theta^k, \theta^{k+1} \in \Theta} \sum_{\phi^k, \phi^{k+1} \in \Phi} \kappa_{AT}(\theta^{k+1}, \phi^{k+1}|\theta^k, \phi^k)$ $o(s^k|\theta^k, \phi^k)o(s^{k+1}|\theta^{k+1}, \phi^{k+1})b(\theta^k, \phi^k)$. The sequence of alerts associated with an IDoS attack $(\Theta, \Phi, \mathcal{K}_{AT}, \mathcal{Z})$ is also a Markov renewal process characterized by the 3-tuple $(\mathcal{S}, \mathcal{K}_{CL}, \mathcal{Z})$.

6.5   Model of Human Attention and Alert Inspection

Figure 6.6 provides a zoomed-in version of the cognitive process illustrated by the green box in Fig. 6.4. Despite technical-level alert selection techniques (e.g., alert filtering shown in the black box of Fig. 6.6) greatly reducing the number of alerts, tier-1 human operators are burned out and cannot inspect all alerts in real-time. According to [5], approximately 23% and 30% of notifications are ignored by cybersecurity teams at businesses with 5000+ employees and 1500–4999 employees, respectively. If an alert is not inspected, it receives the label w_{NI}.

As an operator starts to investigate an alert, he also needs to divide his attention among newly-arrived alerts and probabilistically switches to new alerts without completing the current investigation. Such switching probability depends on the category label of the current and the new alerts. For example, if the new alert is of much higher criticality and time sensitivity than the old one, then the switching probability is high. We denote $\kappa_{SW}^{\Delta k}(s^{k+\Delta k}|s^k)$ as the operator's default switching probability when the previous alert at attack stage k and the new alert at stage $k + \Delta k$, $\Delta k \in \mathbb{Z}^+$, have category label $s^k \in \mathcal{S}$ and $s^{k+\Delta k} \in \mathcal{S}$, respectively. As a probability measure,

$$\sum_{\Delta k=1}^{\infty} \sum_{s^{k+\Delta k} \in \mathcal{S}} \kappa_{SW}^{\Delta k}(s^{k+\Delta k}|s^k) = 1, \forall k \in \mathbb{Z}^{0+}, \forall s^k \in \mathcal{S}. \tag{6.1}$$

As shown in (6.1), the switching can happen at all future attack stages $\Delta k \in [1, \infty)$ whenever a new alert arrives.

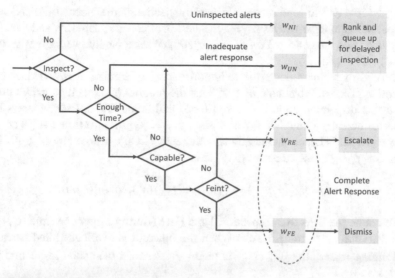

Fig. 6.6 Flowchart of human operators' alert response processes. Given enough time, a capable operator can achieve a complete alert response. Then, he escalates (denoted by w_{RE}) or dismisses (denoted by w_{FE}) the alert based on whether it is a feint or not. Uninspected alerts and alerts of inadequate response, denoted by w_{NI} and w_{UN}, respectively, are ranked and queued up for delayed inspection

Switching Probability

The switching probability affects whether a new alert is inspected and the total time of investigation for the current alert, as illustrated by the first two rhombuses in Fig. 6.6.

As long as an operator is investigating an alert, his attention can change dynamically. The persistent arrival of new alerts can distract his attention, increase his stress level, and affect the efficiency of the investigation. We consider the following attention factors that affect operators' alert investigation and response processes.

- The operator's expertise level denoted by $y_{EL} \in \mathcal{Y}_{EL}$.
- The k-th alert's category label $s^k \in \mathcal{S}$.
- The k-th attack's type θ^k and target ϕ^k.
- The operator's stress level $y^t_{SL} \in \mathbb{R}^+$, which changes with time t as new alerts arrive.

The first three factors are the static attributes of the analyst, the alert, and the IDoS attack, respectively. They determine the average inspection time, denoted by $\bar{d}(y_{EL}, s^k, \theta^k, \phi^k) \in \mathbb{R}^+$, to reach a *complete response* w_{FE} or w_{RE}. We use

$d(y_{EL}, s^k, \theta^k, \phi^k)$ to represent the Actual Inspection Time Needed (AITN) when the operator is of expertise level y_{EL}, the alert is of category label s^k, and the attack has type θ^k and target ϕ^k. AITN $d(y_{EL}, s^k, \theta^k, \phi^k)$ is a random variable with mean $\bar{d}(y_{EL}, s^k, \theta^k, \phi^k)$.

The fourth factor reflects the temporal aspect of human attention during the inspection process. We denote $n^t \in \mathbb{Z}^{0+}$ as the number of alerts that arrives during the current inspection up to time $t \in [0, \infty)$ and model the operator's stress level y_{SL}^t as an increasing function f_{SL} of n^t, i.e., $y_{SL}^t = f_{SL}(n^t)$. At time $t \in [0, \infty)$, the human operator's Level of Operational Efficiency (LOE), denoted by $\omega^t \in [0, 1]$, is a function f_{LOE} of the stress level y_{SL}^t, i.e.,

$$\omega^t = f_{LOE}(y_{SL}^t) = (f_{LOE} \circ f_{SL})(n^t), \forall t \in [0, \infty). \tag{6.2}$$

We define the Effective Inspection Time (EIT) during inspection time $[t_1, t_2]$ as the integration $\tilde{\omega}^{t_1, t_2} := \int_{t_1}^{t_2} \omega^t dt$. When the operator is overloaded and has a low LOE during $[t_1, t_2]$, the EIT $\tilde{\omega}^{t_1, t_2}$ is much shorter than the actual inspection time $t_2 - t_1$.

Suppose that the operator of expertise level y_{EL} inspects the k-th alert for a duration of $[t_1, t_2]$. If the EIT has exceed the AITN $d(y_{EL}, s^k, \theta^k, \phi^k)$, then the operator can reach a complete response w_{FE} or w_{RE} with a high success probability denoted by $p_{SP}(y_{EL}, s^k, \theta^k, \phi^k) \in [0, 1]$. However, when $\tilde{\omega}^{t_1, t_2} < d(y_{EL}, s^k, \theta^k, \phi^k)$, it indicates that the operator has not completed the inspection, and the alert response concerning the k-th alert is $w^k = w_{UN}$. The success probability p_{SP} depends on the operator's capacity to identify attack types, which leads to the definition of the capacity gap below.

Definition 6.1 (Capacity Gap) For an operator of expertise level $y_{EL} \in \mathcal{Y}_{EL}$, we define $p_{CG}(y_{EL}, s^k, \theta^k, \phi^k) := 1 - p_{SP}(y_{EL}, s^k, \theta^k, \phi^k)$ as his capacity gap to inspect an alert with category label $s^k \in \mathcal{S}$, type $\theta^k \in \Theta$, and target $\phi^k \in \Phi$.

Attention Factors
The four attention factors indirectly determine whether the current alert has enough time for investigation, as denoted by the second rhombus in Fig. 6.6. In particular, the first three determine the AITN, while the fourth affects the EIT by affecting the human operator's LOE. An alert has sufficient investigation time if EIT is greater than AITN.

Capacity Gap
The capacity gap probabilistically determines whether the operator is sufficiently capable, as denoted by the third rhombus in Fig. 6.6, to investigate the current alert to achieve a complete alert response.

6.6 Model of AI-Powered Enhancer

Following Sect. 6.5, the frequent arrival of alerts can overload human operators, reduce their LOE that leads to a shorter EIT. The basic idea of the AI-powered enhancer follows the "less is more" principle to apply *cognitive-level* alert selection illustrated in the blue box of Fig. 6.4. We can intentionally make some alerts less noticeable, e.g., without sounds or in a light color, based on their category labels and attention dynamics, to compensate for the attention limitations of the human operators.

In this work, we focus on the class of Attention Management (AM) strategies, denoted by $\mathcal{A} := \{a_m\}_{m \in \{0,1,\cdots,M\}}$, that de-emphasize consecutive alerts. Since the operator can only inspect some alerts in real time, we use $I_h \in \mathbb{Z}^{0+}$ and $t^{I_h} \in [0, \infty)$ to denote the index and the time of the alert under the h-th inspection; i.e., the inspection stage $h \in \mathbb{Z}^{0+}$ is equivalent to the attack stage $I_h \in \mathbb{Z}^{0+}$. Whenever the operator starts a new inspection at inspection stage $h \in \mathbb{Z}^{0+}$, RADAMS determines the AM action $a^h \in \mathcal{A}$ for the h-th inspection based on the stationary strategy $\sigma \in \Sigma : \mathcal{S} \mapsto \mathcal{A}$ that is adaptive to the category label of the h-th alert.

We illustrate the timeline of the AM strategies in blue in Fig. 6.5. The non-transparent and semi-transparent blue arrows indicate the emphasized and de-emphasized alerts, respectively. At inspection stage h, if $a^h = a_m$, RADAMS will make the next m alerts less noticeable; i.e., the alerts at attack stages $I_h + 1, \cdots, I_h + m$ are de-emphasized. Denote $\bar{\kappa}_{SW}^{I_{h+1}-I_h, a^h}(s^{I_{h+1}}|s^{I_h})$ as the operator's switching probability to these de-emphasized alerts under the AM action $a^h \in \mathcal{A}$. Analogously to (6.1), the following holds for all $h \in \mathbb{Z}^{0+}$ and $a^h \in \mathcal{A}$, i.e.,

$$\sum_{I_{h+1}=I_h+1}^{\infty} \sum_{s^{I_{h+1}} \in \mathcal{S}} \bar{\kappa}_{SW}^{I_{h+1}-I_h, a^h}(s^{I_{h+1}}|s^{I_h}) \equiv 1, \forall s^{I_h} \in \mathcal{S}. \tag{6.3}$$

The deliberate de-emphasis on selective alerts brings the following tradeoff.

- These alerts do not increase the operator's stress level, and the operator can pay sustained attention to the alert under inspection with high LOE and EIT.
- These alerts do not draw the operator's attention, and the operator is less likely to switch to them during the real-time monitoring and inspections.

For each alert at attack stage $k \in \mathbb{Z}^{0+}$, RADAMS assigns a stage cost $\bar{c}(w^k, s^k) \in \mathbb{R}$ to evaluate the outcomes of alert response $w^k \in \mathcal{W}$ under the category label $s^k \in \mathcal{S}$. When the operator starts a new inspection at inspection stage $h + 1$, RADAMS evaluates the effectiveness of the AM strategy for the h-th inspection. The performance evaluation is reflected by the Expected Consolidated Cost (ECoC) $c : \mathcal{S} \times \mathcal{A} \mapsto \mathbb{R}$ at each inspection stage $h \in \mathbb{Z}^{0+}$. We denote the realization of $c(s^{I_h}, a^h)$ as the Consolidated Cost (CoC) $\tilde{c}^{I_h}(s^{I_h}, a^h)$. Since the AM strategy σ at each inspection stage can affect the future human inspection process and the alert responses, we define the Expected Cumulative Cost (ECuC) $u(s^{I_h}, \sigma) := \sum_{h=0}^{\infty} \gamma^h c(s^{I_h}, \sigma(s^{I_h}))$ under adaptive strategy $\sigma \in \Sigma$ as the long-term performance measure. The goal of the assistive technology is to design the optimal adaptive strategy $\sigma^* \in \Sigma$ that minimizes the ECuC u under the presented IDoS attack based on the category label $s^{I_h} \in \mathcal{S}$ at each inspection stage h. We define $v^*(s^{I_h}) := \min_{\sigma \in \Sigma} u(s^{I_h}, \sigma)$ as the optimal ECuC when the category label is $s^{I_h} \in \mathcal{S}$. We refer to the *default AM strategy* $\sigma^0 \in \Sigma$ as the one when no AM action is applied under all category labels, i.e., $\sigma^0(s^{I_h}) = a_0, \forall s^{I_h} \in \mathcal{S}$.

Due to the absence of the following exact model parameters, RADAMS has to learn the optimal AM strategy $\sigma^* \in \Sigma$ based on the operator's alert responses in real time.

- Parameters of the IDoS attack model (e.g., κ_{AT} and z) in Sect. 6.3 and the alert generation model (e.g., o) in Sect. 6.4.
- Parameters of the human attention model (e.g., f_{LOE} and f_{SI}), inspection model (e.g., $\kappa_{SW}^{\Delta k}$, $\bar{\kappa}_{SW}^{I_{h+1} - I_h, a^h}$, and d), and alert response model (e.g., y_{EL} and p_{SP}) in Sect. 6.5.

Define $Q^h(s^{I_h}, a^h)$ as the estimated ECuC during the h-th inspection when the category label is $s^{I_h} \in \mathcal{S}$ and the AM action is a^h, we have the following Q-learning equation, i.e.,

$$
\begin{aligned}
Q^{h+1}(s^{I_h}, a^h) := & (1 - \alpha^h(s^{I_h}, a^h)) Q^h(s^{I_h}, a^h) \\
& + \alpha^h(s^{I_h}, a^h)[\tilde{c}^{I_h}(s^{I_h}, a^h) + \gamma \min_{a' \in \mathcal{A}} Q^h(s^{I_{h+1}}, a')],
\end{aligned}
\tag{6.4}
$$

where s^{I_h} and $s^{I_{h+1}}$ are the observed category labels of the alerts at the attack stage I_h and I_{h+1}, respectively. We illustrate the adaptive learning loop of the optimal AM strategy to combat IDoS attacks in Fig. 6.7.

Algorithm 2 illustrates the steps to learn the adaptive AM strategy based on the operator's real-time alert monitoring and inspection process. Each simulation run corresponds to the operator's work shift of 24 h at the SOC. Since the SOC can receive over 10 thousand of alerts in each work shift, we can use infinite horizon to approximate the total number of attack stages $K > 10,000$. Whenever the operator starts to inspect a new alert at inspection stage I_{h+1}, RADAMS applies Q-learning in (6.4) based on the category label $s^{I_{h+1}}$ of the newly arrived alert and determines the AM action a^{h+1} for the $h + 1$ inspection based on the ϵ-greedy policy as shown

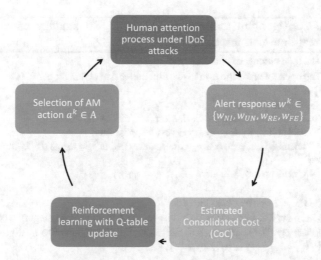

Fig. 6.7 The adaptive learning loop of the optimal AM strategy against IDoS attacks. Based on the operator's performance on alert response, the AM strategy learns to de-emphasize alerts in real time to reduce the cognitive load and improve the CoC of the alert response process

in lines 12 and 19 of Algorithm 2. The CoC $\tilde{c}^{I_h}(s^{I_h}, a^h)$ of the h-th inspection under the AM action $a^h \in \mathcal{A}$ and the category label s^{I_h} of the inspected alert can be computed iteratively based on the stage cost $\bar{c}(w^k, s^k)$ of the alerts during the attack stage $k \in \{I_h, \cdots, I_{h+1} - 1\}$, as shown in lines 13, 20, and 24 of Algorithm 2.

6.7 Conclusions and Future Work

IDoS attacks generate a large number of feint attacks on purpose to deplete the limited human attention resources and exacerbate the alert fatigue problem. In this chapter, we have formally defined IDoS attacks as a sequence of feint and real attacks of heterogeneous targets, which can be characterized by the Markov renewal process. We have abstracted the alert generation and technical-level triage processes as a revelation probability to establish a stochastic relationship between the IDoS attack's hidden types and targets and the associated alert's observable category labels. We have explicitly incorporated human factors (e.g., levels of expertise, stress, and efficiency) and empirical results (e.g., the Yerkes–Dodson law and the sunk cost fallacy) to model the operators' attention dynamics and the processes of alert monitoring, inspection, and response in real time. Based on the system-scientific human attention and alert response model, we have developed a Resilient and Adaptive Data-driven alert and Attention Management Strategy (RADAMS) [2, 3] to assist human operators in combating IDoS attacks. We have proposed a RL-based algorithm to obtain the optimal assistive strategy according to the costs of the operator's alert responses in real time.

Algorithm 2: Algorithm to learn the adaptive AM strategy based on the operator's real-time alert inspection

---

1 Input K: The total number of attack stages;
2 Initialize The operator starts the h-th inspection under AM action $a^h \in \mathcal{A}$; $I_h = k_0$;
    $\tilde{c}^{I_h}(s^{I_h}, a^h) = 0$;
3 for $k \leftarrow k_0 + 1$ **to** K **do**
4   **if** *The operator has finished the I_h-th alert (i.e., EIT > AITN),* **then**
5   **if** *Capable (i.e., rand $\leq p_{SP}(y_{EL}, s^k, \theta^k, \phi^k)$)* **then**
6 | Dismiss (i.e., $w^{I_h} = w_{FE}$) or escalate (i.e., $w^{I_h} = w_{RE}$) the I_h-th alert;
7   **else**
8 | Queue up the I_h-th alert, i.e., $w^{I_h} = w_{UN}$;
9   **end**
10 $\tilde{c}^{I_h}(s^{I_h}, a^h) = \tilde{c}^{I_h}(s^{I_h}, a^h) + \bar{c}(w^{I_h}, s^{I_h})$;
11 $I_{h+1} \leftarrow k$; The operator starts to inspect the k-th alert with category label $s^{I_{h+1}}$;
12   Update $Q^{h+1}(s^{I_h}, a^h)$ via (6.4) and obtain the AM action a^{h+1} by ϵ-greedy policy;
13 $\tilde{c}^{h+1}(s^{I_{h+1}}, a^{h+1}) = 0$; $h \leftarrow h + 1$;
14   **else**
15   **if** *The operator chooses to switch **or** The MAD is reached, i.e.,*
          $t^k - t^{I_h} \geq D_{max}(s^{I_h})$ **then**
16   Queue up the I_h-th alert (i.e., $w^{I_h} = w_{UN}$);
17 $\tilde{c}^{I_h}(s^{I_h}, a^h) = \tilde{c}^{I_h}(s^{I_h}, a^h) + \bar{c}(w_{UN}, s^{I_h})$;
18 $I_{h+1} \leftarrow k$; The operator starts to inspect the k-th alert with category label
          $s^{I_{h+1}}$;
19   Update $Q^{h+1}(s^{I_h}, a^h)$ via (6.4) and obtain the AM action a^{h+1} by ϵ-greedy
          policy;
20 $\tilde{c}^{h+1}(s^{I_{h+1}}, a^{h+1}) = 0$; $h \leftarrow h + 1$;
21   **else**
22   The operator continues the inspection of the I_h-th alert with decreased LOE;
23   The k-th alert is queued up for delayed inspection (i.e., $w^k = w_{NI}$);
24 $\tilde{c}^{I_h}(s^{I_h}, a^h) = \tilde{c}^{I_h}(s^{I_h}, a^h) + \bar{c}(w_{NI}, s^k)$;
25   **end**
26   **end**
27 end
28 Return $Q^h(s, a), \forall s \in \mathcal{S}, a \in \mathcal{A}$;

The future work would incorporate more generalized models (e.g., the spatio-temporal self-excited process) to capture the history-dependent temporal arrival of IDoS attacks, the spatial location of the alerts, their impacts on human attention, and the associated human-assistive security technologies.

References

1. Hassan WU, Guo S, Li D, Chen Z, Jee K, Li Z, Bates A (2019) Nodoze: combatting threat alert fatigue with automated provenance triage. In: Network and distributed systems security symposium

2. Huang L, Zhu Q (2021) Combating informational denial-of-service (IDoS) attacks: modeling and mitigation of attentional human vulnerability. In: International conference on decision and game theory for security. Springer, Cham, pp 314–333
3. Huang L, Zhu Q (2022) Radams: resilient and adaptive alert and attention management strategy against informational denial-of-service (IDoS) attacks. Comput Secur 121:102844
4. Koucham O, Mocanu S, Hiet G, Thiriet JM, Majorczyk F (2022) Cross-domain alert correlation methodology for industrial control systems. Comput Secur 118:102723
5. Robinson C (2021) In cybersecurity every alert matters. Tech. rep., IDC research
6. Vaccine Makers Project (2017) How does hepatitis B combat the immune system? https://vimeo.com/248010182
7. Zhong C, Yen J, Liu P, Erbacher RF (2018) Learning from experts' experience: toward automated cyber security data triage. IEEE Syst J 13(1):603–614
8. Zimmerman C (2014) Ten strategies of a world-class cybersecurity operations center. The MITRE Corporation

Chapter 7
Summary and Conclusions

Abstract This book has introduced emerging cyber threats that exploit human vulnerabilities to obtain initial credentials from human users. Cognitive security is a primary concern that needs to be addressed in HCPSs. We have presented a system-scientific foundation that builds on and bridges the fields of psychology, neuroscience, data science, decision theory, and game theory. Such a foundation has led to transdisciplinary socio-technical solutions that protect humans from cognitive security threats and improve the resiliency of HCPSs. In this chapter, we summarize the book, discuss several insights, explore potential applications, and suggest potential directions for future work.

Keywords Theory of security mind · Trustworthy HCPS · Cognitive digital twins · Cyber decision dominance · Bilateral cognitive game · Socio-economic cybersecurity

7.1 Summary and Insights

Protecting Cyber-Physical System (CPS) from sophisticated attacks, including Advanced Persistent Threat (APT) and supply chain attacks, is critical to national security. A rich literature has focused on threats from the cyber and physical domains, but comparably less ample literature has investigated the impact of the indispensable human factors in CPS security. With the recent advances in Industry 5.0 and the Internet of Things, the complexity of CPS has been growing, and their interactions with humans are omnipresent and increasingly pervasive. This growth significantly increases the attack surface of the system and galvanizes security concerns, especially those that arise from human vulnerabilities. This book has focused on a class of human vulnerabilities that are inherently associated with the cognitive processes of humans.

It is challenging to model, quantify, and control human behaviors and their cognitive processes (e.g., reasoning, perception, and cognition) in CPSs. This book provides a system-scientific perspective that focuses on the system-level stimuli-

© The Author(s), under exclusive license to Springer Nature Switzerland AG 2023
L. Huang, Q. Zhu, *Cognitive Security*, SpringerBriefs in Computer Science,
https://doi.org/10.1007/978-3-031-30709-6_7

behavior relationships to characterize and mitigate human cognitive vulnerabilities, prevent them from adversarial exploitation, and ultimately harden cognitive security.

Previous works on HCPS security have centered around either *big models* or *big data*. The goal of the big models is to create sophisticated and comprehensive modeling based on acquired information and knowledge to inform decision-making, e.g., [26, 51, 53], while the big data approach aims to dispense with abstractions and modeling and make use of the abundance of data to provide insights and achieve design objectives, e.g., [37, 39, 47]. System science goes beyond them and views HCPSs from the lens of systems. It enables us to develop *human-technical* solutions and extract *deep intelligence* (represented by incisive laws and principles) from human behavior and biometric data. The system science view of human systems can be traced back to the earlier years of the development of cybernetics, where feedback system principles have been applied to study biological, cognitive, and social systems [54]. Security introduces a new dimension of system attributes, distinguished by adversarial behaviors and their interactions with the system. The system-scientific approach allows us to focus on the appropriate level of abstraction of the security problem and not be sidetracked by the fine-grained details of the complex systems, such as the biochemical processes in the brain and the microscopic dynamics of the physical systems. In this way, we can create appropriate metrics, relevant insights, and fundamental principles.

After a succinct review of human cognitive capabilities in Chap. 3 and cognitive vulnerabilities in Chap. 4, we have focused on attentional vulnerabilities and introduced ADVERT [27] in Chap. 5 and RADAMS [24, 25] in Chap. 6 to defend against reactive and proactive attention attacks, respectively. Both ADVERT and RADAMS have established data-driven mechanisms that take into account human vulnerabilities (e.g., bounded attention) and assist humans (e.g., users and operators) in deterring and correcting their misbehaviors in an adaptive manner. They have laid the foundation for the *theory of security mind* by characterizing the human cognitive processes in CPS to make the human-assistive mechanisms *Reliable, Explicable, Approachable*, and *Legible*, which we refer to as the *REAL* design principle.

The system-scientific methods used in these two cognitive security models can be generalized and transferred to a broader class of HCPS applications. For example, ADVERT would be applicable to web phishing [14, 55], autonomous driving [15, 17], and other security scenarios where inattention can lead to great threats, and proper perception aids are necessary to mitigate inattention. RADAMS would be useful for healthcare [4], public transport control [33], and weather warnings [50] that require human operators with limited attention resources to monitor and manage massive alerts in real time with a high level of situational awareness.

Chapters 5 and 6 have considered non-strategic cognitive attack models who exploit attention vulnerabilities in a prescribed way, either reactively or proactively. The attacker is not assumed to be strategic or adaptive with the capability of online reasoning, enabled by human or machine intelligence. It would be possible for attackers who exploit cognitive vulnerabilities to adopt adaptive and stealthy strategies. For example, an attacker can learn from the human response and adapt the phishing strategies over time, or an attacker can continuously monitor the attention of the victim and constantly create camouflage or deception mechanisms to steer the victim's attention.

Game-theoretic models become appropriate tools to capture the strategic behaviors of the attacker and their interactions with the human-centered system [36, 46]. The cognitive models can incorporate the game-theoretic description of the attacker, as introduced in Sect. 2.2, into the analysis and design of the defense strategy. This approach has a strong connection with recent endeavors in cyber deception [23, 41, 45, 46]. The research on cyber deception has primarily focused on the development of deception and counterdeception technologies, including honeypots [21, 22], misinformation [20, 49], obfuscation [42, 44], and perturbation methods [40, 43], to mislead the decision-making process of the attacker and hence create an information advantage for the defender.

It has been recently noted in the research community [8] that humans are not a removable component in cyber deception. For example, biasing the users to trust an information item or instilling in the form of phishing email [12, 27] or fake news [6, 30] would result in implanting undetectable malware within the network. One key message of this book is to alert us to the fact that human cognitive processes have inherent vulnerabilities and lead to fallacious reasoning and unreliable security decisions, but what exacerbates the situation is that an attacker can intentionally exploit them and elicit an outcome in favor of the attacker. Hence there is a need to strengthen the security designs with a consolidated understanding and modeling of human perception and cognition. To this end, game theory is an appropriate approach that can incorporate a variety of human factors [7, 10, 13] and achieve a holistic framework for system-level analysis and design.

7.2 Applications in Trustworthy HCPS

Cognitive security is an essential component for constructing trustworthy HCPSs of ubiquitous intelligence. The applications include secure SOC [38], autonomous driving [48], human-robot teaming [35], and telesurgery [34], where attacks can exploit human cognitive vulnerabilities and cause life-threatening impacts. As the human role in different applications varies, the focus of security concerns regarding human vulnerabilities also differs. For example, in telesurgery systems, a robotic surgical system is remotely controlled by a surgeon, who plays a leading role in performing surgery on a patient, while information systems act as a supporting role to achieve the goal of the surgeon. Manipulating the attention or delaying the information system can mislead the surgeon and lead to inaccurate decisions and medical errors. In human-robot teaming problems, human workers and robots collaborate on tasks, for example, in a warehouse or on the battlefield. Human agents can be misled by an adversary and are unable to detect anomalies when there is an intruder or a terrorist. The failure of the detection can propagate, exacerbate, and cause the entire team to fail. It is of paramount importance to understand cognitive security by creating general scientific approaches that can characterize, analyze, and mitigate cognitive attacks.

The effort of system-level modeling of human attention in this book is a preliminary step toward a comprehensive modeling of human cognitive processes. With the growing efforts of the research community, it is possible for us to construct digital twins of human users, operators, and administrators that can represent the system-level cognitive behaviors of human agents. The *cognitive digital twins* enable a modular, flexible, and multi-scale representation of human body signs, emotions, and consciousness. For example, a cognitive digital twin can be composed of hierarchical building blocks of perception, attention, memory, and mental operation, where each building block builds on lower-level building blocks that can be assembled for various functions under different scenarios. One advantage of the cognitive digital twin is its integration with the cyber-physical digital twins. The integration enables the simulation and visualization of various contingent threat scenarios. It would lead to a comprehensive vulnerability and risk analysis of cognitive scenarios and an improved security assessment and design.

Another advantage of the cognitive digital twin is that it would enable the development of customizable security training and mitigation strategies for human users. For example, in the context of attentional vulnerabilities, we have developed mitigation strategies relying on the introduction of signals and alerts to influence or guide human attention. The development of cognitive digital twins can build on the recent advances in Virtual Reality (VR) and Augmented Reality (AR) technologies to create customizable VR/AR-based cognitive interfaces [1, 2]. The technology would be used to train human operators to deal with a variety of cognitive threats using simulated scenarios. It would be further developed into wearable devices that can augment human attention when humans team with machines in mission-critical tasks, such as those on the battlefield and in critical infrastructures.

7.3   Cognitive Insecurity of Adversaries

The research presented in this book is motivated by the cognitive vulnerabilities of the defender. Attackers are also humans and possess the same classes of vulnerabilities. It would be possible to design a sophisticated defense that leverages attackers' cognitive processes to safeguard networks. Proactive mechanisms, such as moving target defense [28, 56] and cyber deception [29, 45], aim to affect attacker perception and behavior to waste time, resources, and mental effort of the attackers. In this way, the defender can mitigate the disadvantages that arise from the asymmetries in knowledge and resources. Several works [16, 19] recently have conducted controlled experiments to investigate the effect of decoys on attacker strategies. It has shown promising results that an attacker's cognition, decision-making, and behavior can be influenced by increasing cognitive biases and introducing uncertainties. The possible disruption of the cognitive processes of the attacker would enable a new type of defense that would trigger early warnings on zero-day APTs and improve the network's defensive posture.

The exploitation of cognitive vulnerabilities would lead to a new battleground for the arms race in cybersecurity. The defender would benefit from developing methods to protect the network from cognitive attacks while creating proactive ways to use cognitive vulnerabilities to deter attackers. As the arms race goes on repeatedly, it would strengthen the defender's capability to make use of AI and learning methods to adapt the mechanism and make strategic decisions that are sufficiently more intelligent and faster than the opponent. It is also known as *cyber decision dominance* [18, 32].

Research in this book has focused on the modeling and analysis of defenders' cognitive processes. To understand the arms race and create decision-dominant solutions, we would need to create a holistic picture by bringing in the attacker's cognitive processes. Hence, there are two competing cognitive processes, and one influences the other. A human-aware game-theoretic analysis of the two cognitive processes would become possible and necessary for creating a promising scientific underpinning to evaluate the cognitive risks, predict outcomes, and design best-effort strategies. It is important to distinguish it from the game-theoretic analysis on a *single cognitive process* pointed out earlier in Sect. 7.1, where the game is played between an attacker who aims to exploit the defender's cognitive vulnerabilities while the defender develops a cyber-physical defense against it. Here, the attacker-defender interaction goes beyond one cognitive process. Players need to create both offensive and defensive strategies to achieve their goals. We call it a *bilateral cognitive game*, which is illustrated in Fig. 7.1.

Fig. 7.1 The interaction between two cognitive processes leads to a bilateral cognitive game. The attacker can create stimuli to manipulate the cognitive process of the defender, while the defender can influence the attacker's cognitive process using deception

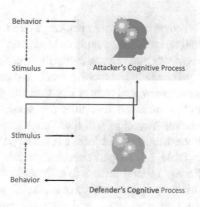

7.4 Expanding the Scope of Cognitive Security

In Sects. 7.4.1, 7.4.2, and 7.4.3, we envision three future directions that would extend the breadth, abundance, and depth of cognitive security, respectively. These guidelines have the potential to advance the research frontier of human cognition and its effects on HCPSs, allowing for a faster convergence of human, cyber, and physical systems.

7.4.1 Breadth: Multi-Dimensional Cognitive Processes

In this book, we have focused on attention as the prototypical human cognition. Other cognitive processes can be introduced into the system model as subsystems and analyzed holistically as a system. Many system-scientific methods, such as the feedback and learning at different time-scales in Chap. 5, would be applicable to a wide range of cognitive processes [5, 52]. Many principles and insights are also transferable. For example, RADAMS in Chap. 6 adopts the "less is more" principle by restricting the amount of information processed by the human operators to be within their attention capacities. Such a principle is transferable to other assailable cognitive resources of human operators, including memory, reasoning, and learning capacity.

7.4.2 Abundance: Multifaceted Measures of Cognitive Factors

As shown in previous chapters, system-scientific models incorporate many cognitive factors, including cognitive loads and incentives, which can be affected by different environmental (e.g., security indicator designs) and human factors (e.g., users' security knowledge, expertise level, and prior trust) [31]. Since those cognitive factors are complex and change dynamically under different environments and individuals, multi-dimension measures are needed to provide more complete, accurate, and efficient evaluations of these cognitive factors. For example, the cognitive load can be measured by subjective reports, performance, and biosensor readings, as shown in Table 7.1. In particular, subjective measures include individuals' self-report of directly related factors (e.g., frustration level, effort, and mental demand [3]) and indirectly related factors (e.g., duration judgment ratio[1] [9]). Performance measures (e.g., the time usage and scores during tasks) and measures from biosensors (e.g.,

---

[1] Duration judgment ratio is the ratio between the real time duration and the perceived time duration. It can be used as a measure of the cognitive load as the perceived time duration can be inversely proportional to cognitive loads.

Table 7.1 Three classes of measures for cognitive loads

Subjective measures	Direct self-report
	Indirect self-report
Performance measures	Task score
	Time usage
Biosensor measures	Heart rate and variability
	Eye movements and pupil dilation
	Brain activities

heart rate, heart rate variability, eye movement patterns, pupil dilation, and brain activities) are objective measures.

Each type of measure has its benefits and limitations. Subjective measures are straightforward to implement, yet the perceived cognitive load can be different from the real one. Performance measures are accurate, yet they may heavily depend on tasks. Thus, it is not a transferable measure among different tasks. Biosensor measures are objective and transferable. However, the analysis of the data can be time-consuming, and there is no unified interpretation of the readings. Therefore, the fusion of these subjective and objective measures fosters strengths and leads to a better understanding of cognitive load and other cognitive factors.

7.4.3 Depth: Multi-Level Characterization of Cognitive Security

One fundamental question to ask is what basic elements or building blocks we need to focus on. For example, we focus on elementary particles in high-energy physics, bits in information theory, and DNA in genetics. For cognitive security, the basic element can be traced down to molecules that constitute cells and neurons. Above the molecule level, neuroscience investigates the components of neurons (e.g., dendrites, axons, and cell bodies) and the structure of the neuronal network to understand fundamental operations in the brain, which lead to complex cognition functions, including perception, attention, memory, and decision, varying under different environments. Theories and models at the cognition level attempt to understand and characterize these functions. Finally, an HCPS includes more than a single human. At the societal level, social science provides a fundamental understanding of human interactions and the Theory of Mind (ToM) shown in Sect. 3.3. We also need management science to incentivize humans and facilitate human cooperation. The understanding of society-level cognitive security contributes to the emerging area of *socio-economic cybersecurity* [11].

The multi-level view provides a multi-scale and hierarchical understanding of cognitive security. On the one hand, as we dig into the microscopic view, we gradually open the black box of human decision-making to understand how the stimulus leads to the behaviors in Fig. 6.5. On the other hand, the understanding at different levels is synthesized to form the whole picture of effectively protecting HCPSs from cognitive attacks.

References

1. Alqahtani H, Kavakli-Thorne M (2020) Design and evaluation of an augmented reality game for cybersecurity awareness (cybar). Information 11(2):121
2. Alzahrani NM, Alfouzan FA (2022) Augmented reality (AR) and cyber-security for smart cities—a systematic literature review. Sensors 22(7):2792
3. Ayres P (2017) Subjective measures of cognitive load: what can they reliably measure? In: Cognitive load measurement and application. Routledge, pp 9–28
4. Backman R, Bayliss S, Moore D, Litchfield I (2017) Clinical reminder alert fatigue in healthcare: a systematic literature review protocol using qualitative evidence. Systematic Rev 6(1):1–6
5. Balzer WK, Doherty ME, et al (1989) Effects of cognitive feedback on performance. Psychol Bull 106(3):410
6. Benkler Y, Faris R, Roberts H (2018) Network propaganda: manipulation, disinformation, and radicalization in American politics. Oxford University Press
7. Bernheim BD, DellaVigna S, Laibson D (2019) Handbook of behavioral economics-foundations and applications 2. Elsevier
8. Bishop M, Wang C, Ferguson-Walter K, Fugate S (2021) Introduction to the minitrack on cyber deception and cyber psychology for defense. In: Proceedings of the 54th Hawaii international conference on system sciences, p 1956
9. Block RA, Hancock PA, Zakay D (2010) How cognitive load affects duration judgments: a meta-analytic review. Acta Psychol 134(3):330–343
10. Camerer CF (2011) Behavioral game theory: experiments in strategic interaction. Princeton University Press
11. Carley KM (2020) Social cybersecurity: an emerging science. Comput Math Org Theory 26(4):365–381
12. Cox EB, Zhu Q, Balcetis E (2020) Stuck on a phishing lure: differential use of base rates in self and social judgments of susceptibility to cyber risk. Compr Results Soc Psychol 4(1):25–52
13. Dhami S (2016) The foundations of behavioral economic analysis. Oxford University Press
14. Egelman S, Cranor LF, Hong J (2008) You've been warned: an empirical study of the effectiveness of web browser phishing warnings. In: Proceedings of the SIGCHI conference on human factors in computing systems, pp 1065–1074
15. El Khatib A, Ou C, Karray F (2019) Driver inattention detection in the context of next-generation autonomous vehicles design: a survey. IEEE Trans Intell Transp Syst 21(11):4483–4496
16. Ferguson-Walter KJ, Major MM, Johnson CK, Muhleman DH (2021) Examining the efficacy of decoy-based and psychological cyber deception. In: 30th USENIX security symposium (USENIX Security 21), pp 1127–1144
17. Fletcher L, Zelinsky A (2009) Driver inattention detection based on eye gaze—road event correlation. Int J Robot Res 28(6):774–801
18. Freedberg Jr SJ (2021) Army's New Aim Is 'Decision Dominance'. https://breakingdefense. com/2021/03/armys-new-aim-is-decision-dominance/
19. Gabrys R, Venkatesh A, Silva D, Bilinski M, Major M, Mauger J, Muhleman D, Ferguson-Walter K (2023) Emotional state classification and related behaviors among cyber attackers. In: Proceedings of the 56th Hawaii international conference on system sciences
20. Gehlbach S, Sonin K (2014) Government control of the media. J Public Econ 118:163–171

21. Horák K, Zhu Q, Bošanskỳ B (2017) Manipulating adversary's belief: a dynamic game approach to deception by design for proactive network security. In: International conference on decision and game theory for security. Springer, pp 273–294

22. Horák K, Bošanský B, Tomášek P, Kiekintveld C, Kamhoua C (2019) Optimizing honeypot strategies against dynamic lateral movement using partially observable stochastic games. Comput Secur 87. https://doi.org/10.1016/j.cose.2019.101579

23. Huang L, Zhu Q (2019) Dynamic bayesian games for adversarial and defensive cyber deception. In: Al-Shaer E, Wei J, Hamlen KW, Wang C (eds) Autonomous cyber deception: reasoning, adaptive planning, and evaluation of HoneyThings. Springer International Publishing, Cham, pp 75–97. https://doi.org/10.1007/978-3-030-02110-8_5

24. Huang L, Zhu Q (2021) Combating informational denial-of-service (IDoS) attacks: modeling and mitigation of attentional human vulnerability. In: International conference on decision and game theory for security. Springer, Cham, pp 314–333

25. Huang L, Zhu Q (2022) Radams: resilient and adaptive alert and attention management strategy against informational denial-of-service (IDoS) attacks. Comput Secur 121:102844

26. Huang Y, Chen J, Huang L, Zhu Q (2020) Dynamic games for secure and resilient control system design. Natl Sci Rev 7(7):1125–1141

27. Huang L, Jia S, Balcetis E, Zhu Q (2022) Advert: an adaptive and data-driven attention enhancement mechanism for phishing prevention. IEEE Trans Inf Forens Secur 17:2585–2597

28. Jajodia S, Ghosh AK, Swarup V, Wang C, Wang XS (2011) Moving target defense: creating asymmetric uncertainty for cyber threats, vol 54. Springer Science & Business Media

29. Jajodia S, Subrahmanian V, Swarup V, Wang C (2016) Cyber deception, vol 6. Springer

30. Kapsikar S, Saha I, Agarwal K, Kavitha V, Zhu Q (2020) Controlling fake news by collective tagging: a branching process analysis. IEEE Control Syst Lett 5(6):2108–2113

31. Kelley T, Bertenthal BI (2016) Real-world decision making: Logging into secure vs. insecure websites. Proc USEC 16(10.14722), 1–10

32. Krause ME (2003) Defense horizons. number 23, February 2003. decision dominance: exploiting transformational asymmetries. Tech. rep., National Defense Univ Washington DC Center for Technology and National Security Policy

33. Lee S, Kim JK (2018) Factors contributing to the risk of airline pilot fatigue. J Air Transp Manag 67:197–207

34. Lee GS, Thuraisingham B (2012) Cyberphysical systems security applied to telesurgical robotics. Comput Stand Interfaces 34(1):225–229

35. Li F, Wang C, Mikulski D, Wagner JR, Wang Y (2022) Unmanned ground vehicle platooning under cyber attacks: a human-robot interaction framework. IEEE Trans Intell Transp Syst

36. Manshaei MH, Zhu Q, Alpcan T, Bacşar T, Hubaux JP (2013) Game theory meets network security and privacy. ACM Comput Surv CSUR 45(3):1–39

37. McAlaney J, Hills PJ (2020) Understanding phishing email processing and perceived trustworthiness through eye tracking. Front Psychol 11:1756

38. Muniz J, McIntyre G, AlFardan N (2015) Security operations center: building, operating, and maintaining your SOC. Cisco Press

39. Mathew A (2021) Deep reinforcement learning for cybersecurity applications. Int J Comput Sci Mob Compu 10(12):32–38. https://doi.org/10.47760/ijcsmc.2021.v10i12.005

40. Oh SJ, Fritz M, Schiele B (2017) Adversarial image perturbation for privacy protection a game theory perspective. In: 2017 IEEE international conference on computer vision (ICCV). IEEE, pp 1491–1500

41. Pawlick J (2018) A systems science perspective on deception for cybersecurity in the internet of things. PhD thesis, New York University Tandon School of Engineering

42. Pawlick J, Zhu Q (2016) A stackelberg game perspective on the conflict between machine learning and data obfuscation. In: 2016 IEEE international workshop on information forensics and security (WIFS). IEEE, pp 1–6

43. Pawlick J, Zhu Q (2016) Two-party privacy games: How users perturb when learners preempt. Preprint. arXiv:160303081

44. Pawlick J, Zhu Q (2017) A mean-field stackelberg game approach for obfuscation adoption in empirical risk minimization. In: 2017 IEEE global conference on signal and information processing (GlobalSIP). IEEE, pp 518–522
45. Pawlick J, Zhu Q (2021) Game theory for cyber deception. Springer
46. Pawlick J, Colbert E, Zhu Q (2019) A game-theoretic taxonomy and survey of defensive deception for cybersecurity and privacy. ACM Comput Surv (CSUR) 52(4):1–28
47. Ramkumar N, Kothari V, Mills C, Koppel R, Blythe J, Smith S, Kun AL (2020) Eyes on URLs: Relating visual behavior to safety decisions. In: ACM symposium on eye tracking research and applications, pp 1–10
48. Ren K, Wang Q, Wang C, Qin Z, Lin X (2019) The security of autonomous driving: threats, defenses, and future directions. Proc IEEE 108(2):357–372
49. Roozenbeek J, Van Der Linden S (2019) The fake news game: actively inoculating against the risk of misinformation. J Risk Res 22(5):570–580
50. Saberian S, Heyes A, Rivers N (2017) Alerts work! Air quality warnings and cycling. Resour Energy Econ 49:165–185
51. Sanjab AJ (2018) Security of cyber-physical systems with human actors: theoretical foundations, game theory, and bounded rationality. PhD thesis, Virginia Tech
52. Schiebener J, Brand M (2015) Decision making under objective risk conditions–a review of cognitive and emotional correlates, strategies, feedback processing, and external influences. Neuropsychol Rev 25(2):171–198
53. Shao CW, Li YF (2021) Optimal defense resources allocation for power system based on bounded rationality game theory analysis. IEEE Trans Power Syst 36(5):4223–4234
54. Wiener N (2019) Cybernetics or control and communication in the animal and the machine. MIT Press
55. Xiong A, Proctor RW, Yang W, Li N (2017) Is domain highlighting actually helpful in identifying phishing web pages? Hum Factors 59(4):640–660
56. Zhu Q, Başar T (2013) Game-theoretic approach to feedback-driven multi-stage moving target defense. In: International conference on decision and game theory for security. Springer, pp 246–263

Printed in the United States
by Baker & Taylor Publisher Services